MANAGING CONFLICT IN THE CHURCH

DAVID W. KALE
with Mel McCullough

Beacon Hill Press of Kansas City
Kansas City, Missouri

Copyright 2003
Beacon Hill Press of Kansas City

ISBN 083-411-9374

Printed in the United States of America

Cover Design: Ted Ferguson

Library of Congress Cataloging-in-Publication Data

Kale, David W., 1943-
   Managing conflict in the church / David W. Kale with Mel McCullough.
      p. cm.
Includes bibliographical references (p.   ).
   ISBN 0-8341-1937-4
   1. Church controversies. 2. Church management. 3. Conflict management—Religious aspects—Christianity. I. McCullough, Mel, 1939- II. Title.

BV652.9.K35 2003
250—dc21

                                                                    2003001659

10   9   8   7   6   5   4   3   2   1

CONTENTS

PREFACE

Conflict is a fact of life—even within the church, and it will never be completely eliminated. The two most common responses to conflict are to ignore it and hope it goes away or handle it badly. In either case, the only thing likely to go away is part of your congregation.

Well-managed conflict, on the other hand, is good for your church. Well-managed conflict is a healthy part of a growing, responsive, in-touch church body.

We surveyed more than 40 pastors about their experiences with church conflict. Although we've gone to great lengths to protect the identities of the individuals and the churches involved, you'll recognize the human frailties that lead to conflict and the spiritual triumph that leads to restoration.

We thank the pastors and laypersons who shared their experiences with us, and pray that the Lord will empower you to use the ideas, accounts, and suggestions here to transform your church into a powerful force for good in your community.

1

CONFLICT IN ACTION

The church board members of Broadview Community Church got quite a surprise when they arrived at a meeting their pastor called before church one Sunday morning. They all had known about the meeting for most of the week, but no one knew the purpose of the meeting. If they expected it to be routine, it was anything but that. When they were all assembled, Pastor Al spoke.

"I've called this meeting to show you a questionnaire I intend to require all church members to fill out at the close of the service today. Some of the questions are for the purpose of updating our files on church members. These questions ask a person's address and how long he or she has attended Broadview. Other questions, however, have to do with the lifestyle guidelines in our denominational policy manual. They ask whether a person smokes, drinks alcohol, or goes to the movies. I've become very concerned about reports of members who are living a lifestyle that is not in harmony with those guidelines. This is particularly disturbing to me when I hear it about those who hold positions of leadership in the church. As you know, our annual church board elections are coming up in a few weeks. After looking at the results of this questionnaire, I will instruct our nominating committee that it may consider only those members who are living a life in accord with those guidelines."

Several members immediately raised their hands. They wanted to know who had put the questionnaire together, and the pastor acknowledged that he had done it himself, closely following the denominational policy manual. They asked for more time to look at the questionnaire and discuss it before the pastor passed it out to the membership. Pastor Al asked if any of the board members had a problem with the requirement that church leaders live in accord with the denominational guidelines.

Bob spoke up. "No, I don't, Pastor. But I have to tell you, if people are not living according to those guidelines, I'm not sure this is the way to deal with it. I'm afraid this questionnaire will tear this church apart."

Donna raised her hand. "Pastor, if I understand what you're saying, if my term is up and I check on my questionnaire that I attend movies, I would not be eligible for reelection."

"That's right, Donna, but I know that wouldn't be a problem for you."

Donna shook her head. "I have to agree with Bob. I'm really afraid of what this is going to do to our church. Can't you put this off so we can talk about it?"

> *My letter of resignation from my board position will be on your desk in the morning.*

"If we put it off, we won't be able to do this before the church board elections. That means we'll have to wait another year. We need to address this situation now before we get more people in leadership positions who don't fit the guidelines of our denomination."

When asked if the board was going to vote on the questionnaire, the pastor said that it was not, but that he would not tell the church members that the board had approved it.

"Do you plan to tell them that the results will be used to determine who is eligible for church board elections?" asked Mike.

"By all means," Pastor Al responded. "People need to know how this information will be used."

Wayne stood up and addressed the pastor. "Pastor, I've been a part of this church for over 15 years and on the board for 10. I can't sit idly by and watch you destroy this church, and I don't want my name associated with this questionnaire in any way. My letter of resignation from my board position will be on your desk in the morning. This is wrong, Pastor. I have no objection to you wanting people to live by denominational guidelines, but this is not the way to go about it." Wayne walked out of the meeting.

When Pastor Al proceeded with having church members fill out the questionnaire after the morning service, there was an immediate and strong reaction. Many members could not believe that the pastor was so callous and insensitive. Some of the board members who were losing their positions had given many years of service and thousands of dollars to the church.

Wayne's letter of resignation was on Pastor Al's desk the next morning as promised, along with the resignations of two other key board members. Several families immediately stopped attending. Others who were offended stayed to try to help the church work through the crisis. Later on, many of these families also stopped attending.

Attendance dropped and financial contributions plummeted. Pastor Al was obviously not pleased to see what was happening. However, he was convinced he had made the right decision. If members were going to hold leadership positions in the church, they should be models of the lifestyle guidelines described in the denominational policy manual.

A group of seven or eight families that left the church decided to begin holding Bible studies on their own until they could sort out their options and decide what they were going to do. They didn't want to see their families go without the spiritual nourishment they needed at this time, and they didn't want to lose contact with other families they knew and loved through their church affiliation. Wayne served as the leader of the group, but he felt inadequate to provide spiritual guidance. He decided to call Pastor John, a retired minister of the denomination living in the area who was also a close friend of some members of the group.

Wayne told John about what had happened and asked John if he would be willing to lead a Bible study for the group until a decision could be made about what they were going to do.

John knew that Pastor Al would be very unhappy with him if

he started meeting with the group, but he agreed to do it. When Al found out, he consulted the denominational leader for his area, and they both agreed that as long as John continued to meet with the group, the group was not likely to return to the church. The denominational leader advised Al to call John and request that he stop meeting with the group.

When Al called John to make this request, he informed John that he and the denominational leader both believed that John was contributing to the breakup of the church. John defended his action by saying that he was only giving spiritual guidance to the group while decisions were being made about what the group was going to do.

The conversation ended with Pastor Al threatening to recommend that John's denominational credentials be rescinded.

"Well, I'm sorry about that, Pastor," John told Al in parting, "not just for myself but for you and the church, because you have the opportunity to build a strong, dynamic church at Broadview, and you're in the process of tearing it apart."

The next day Pastor John received a second phone call, this time from Keith, the denominational leader in the area. Keith repeated the request that John discontinue meeting with the families that had left the church. Again, John kindly, but firmly, asserted that he would continue to meet with them until they figured out what they were going to do. Keith set up a time when he and Pastor Al could come to meet with Pastor John at his home. Keith requested that John have his denominational credentials available and that it would be necessary for him to surrender them at that time. The meeting was set up, the three men had a polite but frank discussion, and Pastor John was relieved of his denominational credentials.

Things then went from bad to worse. All of the members who were meeting in the Bible study immediately contacted Al to say they were withdrawing their membership from the church. They and Pastor John also withdrew from the denomination. The group discontinued meeting, and the families went their own ways, mostly joining other denominations. It would be many years before Broadview would return to the size and vitality it had known before the conflict.

Twenty years later, a subsequent pastor of Broadview Community Church who had no part in the conflict heard about the events that had torn apart the congregation in days gone by. He decided a healing service was needed if there was ever to be any binding up of the wounds that the conflict had inflicted upon the congregation. The families that had left the church were invited to come to the service and

Mishandled conflict can wreak havoc in church.

many of them did. While all expressed appreciation for the pastor reaching out to them, none returned to the church or the denomination. It's hard to calculate the long-term damage brought on by this conflict.

While names and some details were changed to protect the identities of those involved, the essential facts have been reported just as they occurred.

Mishandled conflict can wreak havoc in church. People are traumatized and lives are turned upside down. Children and young Christians get a poor image of what the church should be like. The image the church portrays to the community is hardly one that demonstrates Christian love. Mishandled conflict sends the message that the church has no better means of addressing its problems than do groups outside the church. Church leadership ranks are depleted, persons who were instrumental in carrying out the duties of the church leave, and important aspects of the church's work will go undone. The financial support base of the church is drastically eroded. Serious conflict can produce grave, negative effects on the life and ministry of the church and its people. Great harm is done to the work of God and His kingdom.

There wasn't necessarily anything wrong with the Broadview church before the conflict arose. As a matter of fact, the church was really quite healthy, effectively reaching the community with the gospel message.

When the conflict developed, it showed that there were significant differences among members as to what the qualifications should be for leadership positions. The conflict also demonstrated that the congregation didn't have an effective way of identifying and dealing with differences within the church. This is undoubtedly true of many churches.

Conflict can provide an opportunity to grow and develop; it does not have to be equated with illness that weakens the body and must be eradicated.

Differing opinions within a church does not mean that the church is a "sick" organization. Healthy churches exist and prosper while maintaining and managing significant differences among their members. As a matter of fact, the conflict experienced at Broadview presented both pastoral staff and laity with a potentially valuable opportunity for learning and growth.

Conflict can provide an opportunity to grow and develop; it does not have to be equated with illness that weakens the body and must be eradicated. It can be an opportunity to learn about yourself and how you manage under tension. It can be an opportunity to practice new behaviors and assess their relevance to other conflicts (Leas 2001c, 12).

The staff and members of Broadview Community Church could have had very profitable discussions on the lifestyle guidelines in the denominational policy manual. This would have permitted all parties to express their perspectives while also learning the views of others. These discussions would have helped the members of Broadview know and understand each other better. People could have learned that deeply committed members will sometimes disagree with other deeply committed members.

How differently this would have turned out if Pastor Al had announced that there was to be an open forum to discuss the lifestyle guidelines in the denominational policy manual. The stated purpose for the discussion could be to determine what role those guidelines would have in upcoming church elections. This was an outstanding opportunity for that role to be determined from within the membership itself rather than imposed by congregational authority. This opportunity was lost, however, because the conflict was mismanaged.

This is not to say that after those discussions there would not have been some members leave the church. Some members may have understood those guidelines in a new way. Others may have discovered there was strong support for the guidelines. Still others may have realized that they had little chance of getting leadership positions in the church. Any one of these people could have concluded that there was a better fit for them in another denomination and left the church. If that had happened, however, they would have left with much better feelings about the pastor and the denomination and with fewer feelings of resentment and hostility.

> *Differences should be expected since people come into churches from a wide variety of backgrounds that have determined their attitudes, beliefs, and values.*

"Conflicts are power struggles over differences" (Halverstadt 1991, 4). The fact that these differences exist does not mean that the church is in conflict, however. Differences should be expected since people come into churches from a wide variety of backgrounds that have determined their attitudes, beliefs, and values. They also come with different views on what it means to be "the church." Conflict develops when opinions, positions, and proposals clash with regard to choices the church is making concerning its ministry. If a struggle erupts over whose proposals, positions, and opinions will prevail, the church is in conflict.

Differences in values lie at the heart of the most bitter church conflicts. Some members value structure and order in the church service while others value spontaneity and informality. Some persons value reaching out into the community while others place more value on building up the Body of Christ. Some members value impressive church buildings to attract new people, while others value media outreach.

Our values determine what we believe and how we see the world. Conflicts in church are often centered around the values that are held most dear. When that happens, we can expect the conflicts to be intense, highly emotional, and difficult to resolve.

Both Pastor Al and the members who left Broadway Community Church would probably have said that their goal was to provide the best leadership for the church. The two factions, however, had very different values for determining what makes a person a good church leader.

Pastor Al placed a high value on conformity to denominational lifestyle guidelines. He wanted lay leaders who would model those guidelines as an example to young Christians and to the new people who were coming into the church.

The dissenting members would have put commitment to the church as a local body as their primary value for determining church leadership. They wanted people who demonstrated a willingness to commit their time and resources toward the church's mission. This is not to say that they had no value for following denominational guidelines, but this was not their primary value.

The stage was set for either an in-depth and helpful discussion of the role the guidelines should play in church elections or a hurtful, destructive conflict with long-term, negative consequences for the church.

Another difference at the heart of the conflict in the Broadview case was a difference of opinion as to how church leadership should be selected. There were members who left the church who totally agreed with Pastor Al in putting faithfulness to denominational lifestyle guidelines as nonnegotiable for determining church leadership but differed strongly with the manner in which he chose to implement that value. The value of their friends and colleagues and for what they considered fair treatment of church members took precedence over their value for the denominational guidelines or for the pastor himself. They therefore joined the group of those who left the church. Some members valued their relationship with Pastor John, and they left the denomination because of the way he was treated by the pastor and the denominational official.

A difference in values is *latent* conflict until one or both parties choose to use the power available to them to incorporate those values into the church decision-making process. Pastor Al used his power as the pastor to determine which members met his criteria for church leadership and to keep those who did not meet the criteria off the ballot. The displeased members used their power by withholding resources the church badly needed. When the power struggle begins, church conflict is no longer latent.

Most difficult church conflicts are power struggles over value differences. The value differences spurring most church conflicts today center around worship styles, decision-making processes, methods of interpreting Scripture, just to name a few.

It's important to note that the use of power in working out value differences does not necessarily ensure a negative outcome. If constructive means of addressing their differences had been pursued by both "powers" at Broadview, the church could have generated new power for the achievement of the church's mission. They could have formed stronger relationships in the church's infrastructure on which to build future church growth. They could have developed effective means for dealing with future conflicts that would have resulted in less disruption of the church's work of taking the gospel to a needy world.

Well-handled conflict produces positive energy for a church. It's called *conflict transformation,* and it's a hot topic today. The term was apparently first used by John Burton in 1988 (Dane 1988, 1). What we mean by this term is that the parties to the conflict work through it in such a constructive manner that significant learning and development occurs in the lives of the individuals involved as well as in the church as a whole. God is able to use the openness and vulnerability of both pastor and people to make one new creation empowered by His Spirit to carry out His mission in the world with greater power than they had ever known before.

*FROM THE PASTOR'S DESK** . . . Twenty years after com-
pletion of college and seminary I enrolled in a course on conflict management in a doctor of ministry program. That
course made me wonder how I survived the previous two
decades of pastoral ministry.*

*An old farmer once said, "Go slow. Churches are a lot like
horses. They don't like to be startled or surprised. It causes de-
viant behavior."*

*The congregational battles fought most frequently are not
over theology but over change.*

*Over the years I have used a process that has served me
well whether change affected only a handful of folks or an entire megachurch. The first thing I do with an innovative idea is
test it with a few trusted people who represent a cross section
of the church family. Their reaction will tell me how most people will respond should the change take place. I talk with
church board members, decision makers, and the average
person in the pew to get their feedback.*

*After sensing in a time of prayer the Spirit's prompting, I
recently asked several what they thought about purchasing
the high school across the street from the church, which
would allow for the closing of the street to the north of our
property and enable much-needed expansion of our facilities.
Obtaining a reading from individuals and small groups helped
me prepare for the full-blown presentation and to see what
might have created conflict and controversy. The idea was
"owned" by the people and today the church is using the Family Life Center and Youth Building seven days a week.*

*Pastor Al failed to adequately inform his church board and
to seek the input of the elected leaders or listen to the nominating committee. This administrative flaw alienated a key
segment of the church body. A more constructive leadership
style could have allowed a patient process for settling differences in a way that empowered all the people to use their gifts
and resources to accomplish the maximum Kingdom purpose.*

*"From the Pastor's Desk" sections were authored by Mel McCullough.

2

A CHRISTIAN VIEW OF HEALTHY CONFLICT

B efore we discuss ways to deal with conflict in the church, let's establish a theological foundation for making conflict a constructive part of church life. This foundation incorporates scriptural principles as a means of advancing God's mission in the world. It is humbling that God chooses to do His work through fallen, imperfect people like us. Scripture is clear, however, that this is the role God has for the church and that we are to be His agents of reconciliation to a broken and hurting world. Ask yourself these questions:

1. Are Christians in the church maturing in their faith?
2. Are church members bringing in and ministering to needy people?
3. Are church members demonstrating Christian love for each other?
4. Is the church ministering to the needs in the surrounding community?

Constructive conflict can result in advances in the church's life and ministry. Conflict that is not handled well damages our witness to the world and keeps us from accomplishing the work the Lord has given us to do (Halverstadt 1991, 10). If God's work is to be accomplished effectively when differences arise within the church, it is imperative that we successfully use constructive conflict and curtail the occurrence of destructive conflict.

As we work with people embroiled in church conflict, we must attempt to maximize the positive tendencies they bring to the table and minimize their harmful tendencies (Halverstadt 1991, 7). Each member brings an essential goodness into conflict in the form of God-given interests, talents, and abilities. If conflict is managed effectively, these resources will be essential in bringing a new energy out of church conflict. Members will also sense a great affirmation that results from making a positive contribution to Christ and His kingdom. People who sense that their gifts have been appreciated and used meaningfully to channel conflict into significant church growth will be generous in sharing those resources. They will also support church leadership as pastors and lay leaders attempt to transform the conflict into new sources of power for the church.

Unfortunately, conflict also brings with it temptations to advance selfish personal agendas, often at the expense of others in the church.

One pastor tells of a conflict between two of his parishioners. Each year the church has a special evangelistic outreach initiative to the community, and they were in the process of planning for the upcoming initiative. One of the planning committee members—we'll call her Alice—was new to the congregation, bringing with her a variety of ideas for the evangelistic outreach initiative. Another committee member—we'll call him John—was the layperson who had been in charge of planning and directing the initiative for many years.

The pastor heard from a couple of church members that in a recent planning session John and Alice had a loud and extended argument over how the upcoming evangelistic initiative would be organized. The planning session had not gone well, accomplishing little, and the initiative was to begin in three months. The pastor realized something had to be done soon if this year's initiative was to be successful.

He personally visited John and Alice in their respective homes to discuss their differences during the planning session. Both of them acknowledged that the unfortunate situation had occurred, that little had been accomplished, and that the initiative was not moving forward. The pastor asked each of them to reevaluate their personal commitment to the evangelistic mission of the church. He stressed the importance of the church demonstrating the principle of Christian love and support for each other.

We should not be content with a conflict management style that only manages to somehow keep conflict in check while church members tiptoe around sensitive topics.

The pastor reports that at a fellowship time during a Sunday morning service shortly following his visits, John and Alice were seen hugging each other, and the evangelistic initiative was back on track. By choosing to subordinate their personal agendas, John and Alice were demonstrating the two basic concepts that form the foundation for our theological view of healthy conflict, *transformation* and *community*.

Transformation

Richard Hays, in his book *The Moral Vision of the New Testament*, identifies the concept of a new creation as a central theme of the New Testament. John and Alice demonstrated this commitment to a new creation very well. Their conflict could have resulted in one or both of them pulling out of the planning committee, potentially resulting in the church losing their valuable contributions to making the evangelistic initiative effective. They could have used the planning process as an arena in which to fight out their struggle for leadership, and they could have put more of their energies into defeating the other than into planning an effective campaign. The result not only may have been an unsuccessful campaign but also may have resulted in great damage to the church.

They chose instead to put aside personal agendas and allow God to create something new in them as individuals, in their relationship, and in the work of the church. They became two strong and effective members contributing meaningfully to the leadership of the campaign. The church will grow as this new creation is put to the service of the Lord rather than to their own selfish agendas.

Westerhoff writes that it is precisely this prospect of transformation that makes us so fearful of conflict (2001, 57). There is pain in birth as a new creation is brought into existence in the church. The comfort and predictability of the old way of doing things is now behind us, and we're not really sure what the new life will be like. Will we be able to handle it? Will there be a meaningful place for us?

Neither John nor Alice knew who would end up with the leadership position in the new committee structure, but they were willing to take the chance for the sake of the church.

We should not be content with a conflict management style that only manages to somehow keep conflict in check while church members tiptoe around sensitive topics. This kind of conflict resolution may accomplish nothing more than to restore relationships and conditions to their preconflict state. If the relationship between Alice and John had been merely restored to its preconflict state, Alice would not have made any meaningful contribution to leading the campaign. This could have been a great loss to the church.

Our goal is conflict *transformation* where God is allowed to work through the conflict to bring new life into the church, providing it with power and resources it did not previously have for achieving His commission.

COMMUNITY

Community is a second central theme Hays identifies in the New Testament. He defines community as "what emerges with the blending of the individual gifts of those in the Body of Christ when those gifts are exercised more for the common good than for the individuals themselves" (1996, 196-97). It is important to note that this is a matter of priority. The emphasis on community does not mean that the use of individual gifts results in no benefit to the individual or that individual needs and interests are ignored, but they are secondary to the advancement of the church's mission.

God's plan for the church is that as the church grows so do the individuals within that church.

For transformation conflict to occur, members put the good of the church ahead of their own personal needs and interests. When members are willing to do this, the transforming power of God will often meet their deep personal needs in ways they never anticipated.

When members use their gifts merely to advance their own interests, they are missing out on some of the richest blessings the Lord offers us through the church. Great joy is available to those who give sacrificially of themselves to help their church bring power out of the pain of conflict.

Again, Alice and John demonstrated this commitment to community. They recognized that their gifts were going to be of greatest use if they were directed toward the church's mission to reach others rather than for personal recognition and reward. They learned a lesson that will benefit them and their church for many years to come.

God's plan for the church is that as the church grows so do the individuals within that church. It is a paradox in that only by devoting their gifts to the benefit of others can individuals realize the greatest personal rewards. It should come as no surprise to us, since Christ told us, "If anyone wishes to come after Me, he must deny himself, and take up his cross and follow Me. For whoever wishes to save his life will lose it, but whoever loses his life for My sake and the gospel's will save it" (Mark 8:34-35, NASB).

Practicing community also means depending on others in the

church. This is difficult to do in the midst of a church fight (West-erhoff 2001, 55). In an individualistic society, the tendency is to protect ourselves and be less concerned about the welfare of others. Yet the concept of Christian community dictates that, even in the threatening time of conflict, our gifts are to be directed primarily for the common good and not for ourselves.

Alice and John had to trust each other to work for the good of the church as a whole. They were dependent on each other to not take advantage of this situation to get the upper hand. Alice's gifts had to be offered to the church in support of John's leadership if that was what was best for the campaign. John's leadership position had to be directed toward promoting Alice's ideas and suggestions, perhaps even to the extent of allowing Alice to take over the leadership position on the committee. Community means depending on others to do what is best for the common good.

A youth pastor tells of a conflict he had with the parents of one of his teen group members. The parents expressed their concerns to him about some of the views he was expressing to the teens, particularly those in which the pastor was associating gun ownership with violence in society. The parents were ardent supporters of the NRA and deeply opposed to the youth pastor sharing his views on the topic. They were equally concerned with their son having a youth pastor who held views so completely opposite their own.

As the youth pastor and the parents talked, it became obvious that there were many areas in which they held different opinions. You can imagine the youth pastor's pleasant surprise when the father concluded the conversation by saying, "We still don't agree on much, Howard, but I trust you. I trust your heart" (Friend 1996, 19). This is the essence of Christian community. It is not that we all hold the same views or goals for what we want our church to be. What allows us to put our gifts in service to the church before ourselves is that we trust the hearts of our brothers and sisters in the Lord. Then we can negotiate with each other, knowing that at our core we are all headed in the same direction.

CHARACTERISTICS OF CHRISTIAN COMMUNITY

When Christian community is fully developed, there are at least four characteristics that will be demonstrated: respect, appreciation for diversity of gifts, accountability, and forgiveness.

Respect

Respect in Christian community includes respect for yourself, respect for the rights and views of others, and respect for the common good of the church (Halverstadt 1991, 34-35). Many Christians have been taught that it's wrong to promote one's own interests or draw attention to one's own ideas or beliefs. But we can respect the good that God has put in us and respect the gifts that He has given us by making ourselves available and asserting ourselves into the community.

Keep in mind the distinction between assertiveness and aggressiveness. The *aggressive* person puts forth his or her views with the goal of overpowering or dominating. The *assertive* person wants his or her views to be considered as having equal worth with those of others. It is good to recognize that your position is one of many and all should be given due consideration.

When conflicts arise, many church members are reluctant to speak up when, in fact, this is when the community most needs a wide variety of ideas to consider. While it may be tempting to say, "I'm not getting involved in that fight," new ideas or positions may be sorely needed. Conflict is not necessarily a win/lose situation. Sometimes an exit option is needed as a means of escaping the power struggle between two positions, and the ideas of a bystander may very well provide that option.

A dose of respect for self is needed in order to jump into the fray of conflict. Remember that a bystander's contribution may help the differing factions reframe the situation in a way they had not even considered.

A fully developed Christian community will grasp the concept of respect for others. It's important to remember that everyone involved is created in the image of God and must be treated with the utmost respect. Character assassination, belittling remarks, and deceitful practices that demean the worth of a person for whom Christ died should not be tolerated.

> *The Christian involved in church conflict should have respect for the common good.*

Christians involved in conflict should respect others because Christian love requires it and because every person in the conflict has a truth we need to hear. Failing to respect anyone shuts us out to part of the truth God has put within our community.

Finally, the Christian involved in church conflict should have respect for the common good. The church is the embodiment of Christ in our lives and is deserving of our highest respect. Although we may not always agree with everything the pastor or anyone else in the church says, we can disagree respectfully. Churches will not be torn apart if all members have high respect for their church community and keep protecting and preserving the community as a goal during church conflict.

Diversity

"There are different kinds of gifts, but the same Spirit. There are different kinds of service, but the same Lord. There are different kinds of working, but the same God works all of them in all men. Now to each one the manifestation of the Spirit is given for the common good" (1 Cor. 12:4-7). Of all people, Christians should appreciate the importance of diversity in community.

One of the reasons we avoid conflict is because it highlights our differences. There is comfort in thinking that we all are the same. Many times our acceptance in the church community depends on us being like the others with whom we worship. But the Scripture is clear that while we worship the same God and serve the same Lord, we have different gifts, we serve differently, and we work differently. Have confidence that with the Lord's help we will be able to "fit these pieces into the breathtaking whole God intends if only we are willing to struggle" (Westerhoff 2001, 56).

Paul writes that the differences God has placed within our community are for the common good. There is great strength in community when our variety of gifts all work in service to our mission. Celebrate our diversity and allow each of us to be the unique person the Lord created us to be. To protect diversity is to sometimes encourage conflict, but if handled correctly, it will add great strength to the community.

Accountability

One pastor we spoke with told of members in his church who developed a musical group. Two of the group members were on the church board and one was the Sunday School director. The more the group performed together, the better they became, and soon the group was getting invitations to be part of the Sunday morning worship services in other churches. The musicians informed the pastor that they would be missing church on many Sunday mornings. The pastor asked if they had a limit in mind as to the number of Sundays they would miss each month. They indicated that they did not and that they planned to accept as many invitations as they received. The pastor suggested that in that case the Sunday School director and board members should resign their positions. He indicated that it would be better if people in those positions were regularly in church services. The group members were extremely unhappy with the pastor and began to work toward having the pastor removed from his position.

Accountability is not always a popular concept. The musical group members apparently sensed no accountability to either the pastor or the church.

Accountability issues are a source of frequent church conflicts. A pastor we heard from told of a church board member he confronted about a personal lifestyle issue that was clearly in violation of scriptural principles. He told her he did not see her behavior as a good example in the church, particularly for a board member. Shortly thereafter the woman's husband stopped coming to church altogether, and her children began harassing the pastor's children at school.

Members of Christian community are accountable to each other and to church leadership for the lives they lead. Pastors are accountable to church members and to denominational leadership for their attitudes and actions.

Forgiveness

The pressure of conflict often causes people to say hurtful things they would not say otherwise, and people are often deeply hurt as a result of power struggles.

David Augsburger writes that true forgiveness *re-creates* as well as reconciles. This happens when people release the past, view the present in a new light, and open the future to new possibilities (1992, 282). Em Griffin reports on research he did with college students on forgiveness. When he asked them how they knew another person had forgiven them, a frequent response was "the person mentioned it to me once, but never mentioned it again."* The other person had released the past.

But releasing the past is not enough if transformation is to take place in the relationship and in the church. It is important for both parties to be willing to see others in the conflict in new ways. If individuals can put away the "us vs. them" way of thinking about those with whom they have been fighting, a new relationship can be created that allows both parties to see that they really need each other. Finally, both parties should open themselves to new risks so that the present can be transformed into a new reality that did not exist before. New ways of relating to each other will open up new possibilities for service and ministry. Through forgiveness, conflict can be an agent of transformation that will allow God to "do a new thing" in His church.

---

*Quoted from paper delivered by Em Griffin at a Religious Speech Communication Association convention.

FROM THE PASTOR'S DESK . . . *I was intrigued by the title of a book,* Great Church Fights, *by Leslie Flynn. The book started with the account of a group of children who worked hard to build their own little cardboard clubhouse.*

As they thought about their club rules, they put together three rather useful ones:

1. Nobody act big.

2. Nobody act small.

3. Everybody act medium.

Impressive theology! And pretty good human relations. "Acting medium" is essential for dealing with conflict according to biblical principles. God was saying to His Church, "act medium" when Paul wrote, "Be devoted to one another in brotherly love; give preference to one another in honor" (Rom. 12:10, NASB). Living our scriptural principles in the community of faith is showing grace to one another. The world does not expect to receive grace from human beings. But this is foundational to the Christian's attitude and actions if conflict is to be healthy and well managed in the church.

The pastor who took the risk to interface and build a bridge between John and Alice is to be commended for providing a compelling example of how to preserve community while boldly stretching the church to commit to the missional goals. Such accountability is one of the most demanding jobs of a local pastor.

Early in my ministry I was made aware of a moral issue between a board member and a Sunday School teacher that obviously violated scriptural teaching. Both had families and extended families in the church and were admired for their hard work for the church. Nevertheless, I had to confront the moral failure and request their resignations. A strong lay leader and my denominational supervisor were kept informed, and I sought their advice and counsel.

Some of the families impacted were distant from me and even the services of the church for a few months, but time and events eventually revealed the truth. The significance of the moment of accountability for the health of the local body was revealed when two leaders confessed that they had been dangerously close to moral failures in their own lives, and the courage to speak the truth in love had been the warning they needed to resist the temptation.

The initial conflict became redemptive and transformational in the long term. Such conflict management may not resemble grace at first, but in the long haul God can use it to administer grace at a strategic time in the church's life.

3

SOURCES OF
CHURCH CONFLICT

C ontrary to popular opinion, conflict is not a sign of a weak
church, weak church leadership, or even a need for spiritual
renewal. And conflict isn't necessarily a sign that a church has
spiritual problems. As a matter of fact, it can be a sign that normal, healthy growth—including spiritual growth—is taking place.
Conflict is a normal part of all human organizations, including the
church.

It could be argued that a pastor or lay leader should be concerned if his or her church is completely conflict free. That could
be a sign that, instead of new growth occurring, the old ways of
doing things are going unchallenged and that new ideas are not
part of the church process. Then, if new members bring with them
new ideas, those new ideas can be seen as challenges by those in
power, and conflict is born.

Parsons and Leas go so far as to take the position that healthy
churches *create* tension. It is their opinion that tension helps
churches stay flexible and ready to change. They believe that if a
church lacks the ability to change, it will get stuck in a rut and begin to decline (2001c, 64). As new people come, if the church fails
to adjust to meet their needs, the newcomers will walk in the front
door and right out the back.

Tension in the church not only keeps the church flexible but also can help keep the staff and members current on their problem-solving skills. With fresh problems presenting themselves regular-

> *Without a clear issue to address, the conflict becomes extremely destructive and begins to tear down the Body, leaving behind broken lives, compromised careers, and severed relationships.*

ly, members and staff learn to identify problems quickly and are able to work together to solve them. When problems are solved and their needs are met, people are at home in the church family, and the Lord's kingdom is advanced.

If a church is stuck in the rut of doing the same things in the same way and spearheaded by the same people, no healthy tension is created to stretch its leaders in ways that can meet today's needs. Rick Ryding, former professor of Christian education at Mount Vernon Nazarene University, is fond of saying, "The seven last words of the church are, 'We've never done it that way before.'" Effective problem solving provides fertile soil for new growth.

Those who believe that conflict is a sign of a weak or sinful church tend to deny that conflict exists in their churches. That denial comes at a heavy price because conflict has to be managed if it is to benefit the church. When the conflict is ignored or denied, the opportunity to manage the conflict is lost. The conflict then takes on a life of its own (Pneuman 2001, 51). People forget what they were actually fighting about and before you know it, the conflict is driving the church rather than the church managing the conflict.

Suddenly it's not about the issues anymore; it's about the power struggle itself. Without a clear issue to address, the conflict becomes extremely destructive and begins to tear down the Body, leaving behind broken lives, compromised careers, and severed relationships. The good news is that well-managed conflict can lead to constructive growth and change in a church.

PASTORS' SURVEY

We asked 40 pastors to identify the sources of conflict in their churches. Of the 35 different sources these pastors identified, following are the most frequently mentioned and the number of pastors who included that source in their list:

1. Communication problems (11)
2. Differences over church mission and direction (9)
3. Personality conflicts (7)
4. Family conflicts (i.e., husbands and wives, parents and children, etc.) (6)
5. Competition (5)
6. Interpersonal relationships (5)
7. Misunderstandings (4)
8. Jealousy (3)
9. Turf protection (2)
10. Personal agendas (2)
11. Lack of forgiveness (2)
12. Work distribution in the church (2)

These identified sources fit into three broad categories with the number of times each category was identified:

1. Relationship problems: communication, personality conflicts, family conflicts, interpersonal relationships, competition (28)
2. Spiritual problems: jealousy, lack of forgiveness, carnality, envy (11)
3. Differences over mission and direction (9)

Three important observations can be made regarding these results. The first is that the church's mission and direction was only one of the 35 different sources of conflict pastors identified in the church. All the others had to do with relationship problems and spiritual problems in the community. Although it is likely that some relationship problems are directly related to spiritual problems, there is no doubt that spiritually active and dedicated Christians still have relationship problems.

The second observation is that of the conflict sources identified by the pastors, only 9 out of 48 were related to the church's mission and direction. This means that more than 80 percent of the time pastors believe the conflict in their churches is brought on by relationship and spiritual problems.

The third important observation is what is *not* on the list. Only one pastor was bold enough to take the position that 50 percent of church conflict is caused by defensiveness on the part of the pastor. Not one other pastor mentioned the pastor as a cause of church conflict. We suspect that if lay members had filled out the questionnaire, we would get a different story.

RESEARCHERS' AND CHURCH CONSULTANTS' PERSPECTIVES

While the perspective of pastors on the causes of church conflicts gives us important insight, it is not the only perspective. Those who have served as church consultants and those who have done research on church conflict also have valuable information to share. From their combined experience, the following list of conflict sources emerges.

Communication

Bob has served Main Street Church as senior pastor for more than 20 years. Also on staff are the associate pastor, the youth pastor, and the worship pastor. Josh, the youth pastor, told Bob two weeks ago that he had accepted a position at another church.

Staff meetings had been tense for the past couple of months—ever since Josh took a group of young people to a professional baseball game, and it turned out several of the young people drank alcohol at the game. Bob believed Josh when he said he had no idea they had been drinking until they got in the van to come home. Even though the group was in a stadium that held more than 30,000, Bob felt Josh had not been diligent in overseeing the group.

Amazingly, the drinking incident wasn't widely known throughout the church. Bob and Josh met with the teens' parents to discuss the situation. One of the parents, Allison, was also a board member, but Bob was sure none of the other board members knew of the incident.

At the regular monthly board meeting when Bob announced that Josh would be leaving, Josh was the only staff member who wasn't there.

"The next item on our agenda is not pleasant for me," Bob announced to the board. "Josh has informed me that he will be leaving to accept a position at another church. He will still be working with youth but will have more administrative responsibilities. Josh has basically done a good job for us, and I'm sure all of you know that his isn't an easy job."

Allison was noticeably shaken when Bob announced that Josh would be leaving, and he wondered if she was assuming that Josh had been fired because of the drinking incident. The other board members seemed to accept the announcement at face value. No questions were asked, and Bob offered no further information.

A couple of days later, Bob received a call from a church member saying that Josh was telling people that the pastor had "ripped me up one side and down the other" in the board meeting. Bob was confused. He racked his brain to figure out what he had said that could have been taken that way.

Bob immediately went to Josh's office, walked in, and closed the door.

"Josh, is it true that you're telling people that I ripped you up one side and down the other in the board meeting when I announced your resignation?"

"What I heard is that you were really critical of the job I've done as youth pastor. Is that true?"

"No, that isn't true. I wouldn't do that. Who told you that?"

"That's what Mike (the associate pastor) told me the morning after the board meeting."

"What exactly did he tell you I said? Did he say I ripped you up one side and down the other?"

"Not exactly. He said you didn't have a lot of nice things to say about my work here."

"Well, it's really not correct then to say I ripped you up one side and down the other, is it?"

"Well, you didn't exactly give me a ringing endorsement."

"Even if that is true, Josh, you're telling people I said something that you know I didn't say. That isn't ethical or professional."

Bob then headed immediately to Mike's office, but Mike had already left the office for the day in order to take care of some church banking business. Bob called Mike at home and told him he had an important matter to discuss with him and wondered if he would be willing to come back to the office. Mike agreed, and about 20 minutes later he walked into Bob's office.

"What's up?"

"Mike, a problem has developed over my announcement in the last board meeting that Josh was resigning. Josh tells me that the next morning you told him that I was very critical of his work here as youth pastor. Is that true?"

"Well, that's how I interpreted what you said. You didn't really give him a ringing endorsement."

"But, Mike, I didn't say one critical word about Josh or the work he's done for us. I'm afraid you and Josh have done a lot of damage with your reports about what took place in that meeting. With him telling that story, the teens probably think I fired him. I don't know why you were telling Josh what happened in board meeting anyway."

"I'm sorry, Pastor. It won't happen again."

The situation at Main Street Church demonstrates the sort of communication problems that can occur in church. Maybe Josh sensed that Bob held him responsible for the drinking incident. Then when Mike reported that Bob hadn't given a "ringing endorsement," Josh's imagination filled in the rest. Mike contributed to the problem by passing along his interpretation of what the pastor said. If he thought the pastor wasn't giving Josh his due, he should have taken it up with the pastor rather than reporting it to Josh.

Protecting Confidential Information

Another communication problem that plagues churches is the failure to protect confidential information. Pastors and lay leaders must be clear with members of committees and task forces when discussions are confidential. On the flip side, pastoral staff and church members need to honor that confidentiality when it is called for. Some pastors and lay leaders have members sign a pledge of confidentiality before serving on nominating or search committees.

Release of confidential information can destroy relationships, careers, and people's reputations. A person who fails to respect confidentiality should forfeit his or her right to serve on committees where this is important. If a pastor fails to respect confidentiality, this should be addressed in his or her performance review.

Communication Problems Caused by Conflict

Conflict itself is often the cause of communication difficulties. People in conflict may become overly defensive and put up emotional walls to defend themselves. These walls keep information from coming in and going out, and rumors and misunderstandings abound, intensifying the conflict. Essentially, the conflict starts feeding on itself, becoming more complicated and difficult to resolve.

Pneuman reports that when a church is troubled, the information exchanged between the church staff and the board is often inadequate, causing people to feel they are being deliberately misinformed or that information is being hidden from them. When an "us vs. them" mentality forms and angry words are exchanged, the original issue takes a backseat to which side will win and which side will lose. This fight is much more difficult to resolve.

Power

The pastors who filled out our survey gave many examples of fights in their churches that were basically power struggles—usually over who was going to control what was happening in the church. Here are some examples:

- New people come in and challenge the way things are done.
- Newly elected church officers try to stamp their individuality on their areas of responsibility, producing resistance from those who are affected.
- Young people resent the older people controlling their activities and want to try things not previously allowed.
- The pastor has ideas on how to run the church while the church board thinks it should set the direction.

All of these situations are struggles for control, and they are a common source of church conflict.

> *Power struggles between the pastor and the board or other influential members have the capacity to do great damage to the church's effectiveness and future.*

One pastor reported an intense struggle between a group of older, longtime members and a group of younger, newer members who wanted to see change. While these conflicts appeared on the surface to be about music style, use of liturgy, and other matters of church polity and practice, the underlying issue was a quest for power.

The older members thought the younger members didn't have enough experience to run the church. The younger members thought the older members were out of touch. But the only conflicts addressed were the surface ones, and the underlying conflict was never really resolved. So the conflict kept reappearing in one form or another, and people started leaving the church.

Power struggles between the pastor and the board or other influential members have the capacity to do great damage to the church's effectiveness and future. Some cases result in the pastor or the church members—and sometimes both—leaving the church, seriously disrupting the church's ability to achieve its mission. Other struggles occur over church resources, causing members to withdraw their attendance and their financial support.

An essential ingredient for a sense of community to exist in the church is for members to be accountable to one another. If a power struggle develops from a lack of accountability, the church has some very deep issues to deal with that will challenge its spiritual heart and soul.

Cosgrove and Hatfield make the point that some pastors may resort to political maneuvering to keep those who differ with them on certain issues from getting positions of power in the church (1994, 21). Pneuman makes a similar point by saying that some pastors have been known to "stack the lay leadership of the congregation with folks who support whatever the pastor is trying to lead the church to do and be" (2001, 53).

If those who differ with the pastor perceive that they are routinely excluded from positions of leadership in the church, the pastor can expect either continual, unproductive conflicts or for many creative and insightful people who happen to differ with the pastor to leave the church. Neither of these outcomes will result in the church achieving its potential for ministry, and the church will continually fall short of what the Lord has called it to be.

Value and Need Differences

"Conflicts stemming from incompatible personal values and needs are some of the most difficult to resolve. They often become highly emotional and take on moral overtones. A disagreement about who is factually correct easily turns into a bitter argument over who is morally right" (Whetten and Cameron 1998, 323; see also Halverstadt 1991, 2; Pneuman 2001, 45; and "When Conflict Erupts in Your Church," 15). Almost all of us know of church splits resulting from differences over worship styles such as contemporary music vs. traditional music, theology, social action, evangelism, and so forth, because those involved see these conflicts as being at the core of what the church is about.

Church fights are not about incidentals but rather about the core values on which the church is based.

In these disagreements it is often nearly impossible to reach a compromise that permits everyone to feel as though he or she has had input into the final decision. Either-or fights seldom have a win-win outcome. They almost always produce win-lose or even lose-lose outcomes.

For those involved, church fights are not about incidentals but rather about the core values on which the church is based. And that is exactly why they often turn so nasty.

Need for Respect

"Whatever the surface issues in dispute, the underlying cause of conflict usually lies in the deprivation of basic human needs like love and respect. . . . If disputes resemble the matches that light the fire, the frustration of needs is like the flammable tinder" (Ury 1999, 118).

People often expect their churches to be the place where their basic need for love and respect will be met, particularly if it's not being met at home or at work. One pastor reported about a new convert who was angry when he was not appointed as a Sunday School teacher. He felt the pastor didn't appreciate his gifts, and he started talking to longtime members in an effort to gain their support in putting pressure on the pastor to give him this assignment. Fortunately the veteran members recognized and supported the pastor's position that the new convert needed to mature spiritually before he would be ready to take on a teaching position.

This need for respect is also frustrated when people feel that their opinions are not listened to or valued. Of course, we are all ready to listen to supportive opinions but find it much harder to listen to those who disagree with us. Pastors and lay leaders will want to be very sensitive to the opinions of new people and those who have differing opinions. When people feel shut out, their need for respect is frustrated and the seeds of conflict are planted.

Scarce Resources

"A church system that is losing such resources as money, volunteer work hours, communal self-esteem, or status in the larger community is 'put on edge' emotionally. Parties to conflicts within that system are more likely to displace and act out system tensions and fears on one another" (Halverstadt 1991, 68).

When there is a fixed amount of resources to be distributed throughout an organization and those resources are scarce, this can set off conflict that is generally win-lose in nature. Those who are the losers are not likely to be supportive of the decisions.

Scarcity of resources also sets off self-esteem problems because members wonder why new members are not coming into the church, why current members aren't giving more, or why so few people are volunteering to carry out church activities. This can result in finger pointing at someone else as being the cause of the problem. The resulting resentment can cause conflict that is difficult to pinpoint or resolve. It will be necessary to focus back on the basic mission of the church and away from the defensiveness caused by scarcity of resources.

Change

Change is a source of conflict that was not mentioned by any of the pastors who completed our survey. Perhaps because pastors are often the initiators of change, and they were reluctant to name themselves as a source of conflict in the church. Many books on leadership encourage pastors to make significant changes in the church early in their tenures to demonstrate their ability to provide the leadership the church needs, thus inspiring confidence.

Many books on leadership encourage pastors to make significant changes in the church early in their tenures to demonstrate their ability to provide the leadership the church needs, thus inspiring confidence.

However, new pastors rushing into change frequently produce conflict (Pneuman 2001, 49). Perhaps the change is warranted to move a church away from lethargy and apathy, but the pastor and church leaders should be aware that if the conflict is not handled effectively, it could have negative results such as loss of resources and membership.

FROM THE PASTOR'S DESK . . . *One of the values I have found in attending seminars or reading the literature that analyzes church conflict is realizing not only that conflict is normal in any alive, growing organization but also that such knowledge gives insight into how to classify conflict. It is essential for leaders to pray for wisdom to know if the conflict is more a relational and communication breakdown, a result of sin and spiritual immaturity, or perhaps a basic philosophical/missional difference.*

Perhaps the most memorable conflict in my ministry came while I was a young and inexperienced pastor. The church was growing through outreach to young adults in our community. New converts were being baptized, received into the membership of the church, and finding places of leadership and service in the congregation. A strong and influential leader took me to lunch and told me we could not assimilate so many new members. He further opposed the new building we desperately needed for Christian education and fellowship.

As the pastor and leader who was casting the vision for the future of the church, I had to boldly communicate to the lay leaders and congregation that our church had to continue evangelizing our community and providing space to disciple and fold these new Christians into our church family. Thankfully, the church continued to reach new people for Christ, and the new building was constructed. Pastor Bob could probably have avoided some of the conflict that developed over the resignation of the youth pastor if he had a policy of handling delicate personnel issues in executive session that would have dismissed other church employees like Mike from the meeting. This could have prevented the misrepresentation of how the resignation was handled by the senior pastor. Some conflict can be avoided by carefully planning meetings in a way that anticipates possible misunderstandings that use up the spiritual and relational resources that detract from the church's main purpose.

4

CONFLICT
LEVELS

It's important for church leaders to effectively identify different types of conflict and be equipped to respond accordingly. Speed Leas, in *Moving Your Church Through Conflict,* has contributed greatly to providing insight into different conflict levels and developing understanding and conflict resolution strategies. His book forms the basis for most of the material in this chapter.

ASSUMPTIONS

The concept of conflict levels is based on several assumptions. The first is that **there are differences in conflict levels according to the level of intensity the conflict has achieved.** These levels can be identified by (1) the objectives parties are attempting to achieve and (2) the language they use to talk about the conflict (Leas 2001c, 19). Church leaders should analyze these two factors before deciding on a response.

The second assumption is that **the response of church leaders must be appropriate to the level of conflict.** There are no cookie-cutter approaches to dealing with conflict. The wrong response could make an intense conflict worse.

The third assumption is that **conflict is experienced differently by different people within the same church** (18). Some members may consider the conflict a threat to the church's very existence while others cannot figure out why people are so upset.

The final assumption we will make is that **conflicts do not all start small.** Many pastors assume they will have a chance to deal with all conflicts at low levels, thereby avoiding major upheaval. Unfortunately, this is probably not true.

Leas writes, "I doubt that future researchers will be able to show a predictable pattern of conflict development from easy to difficult. Depending on what is at stake, the level of fear in the system (or individual), the skill with which people manage differences, and other such factors, conflict may begin at high levels without going through easier, lower 'stages'" (18).

CONFLICT LEVELS

In discussing conflict levels, it is important to remember that we are defining conflict as power struggles over differences. Therefore, when church members become aware that they have competing goals or differing opinions, this does not mean they are automatically in conflict.* Based on our definition, then, we will discuss five levels. The first two are really preconflict levels followed by three levels of actual conflict. Our levels are as follows:

1. Awareness of Differences
2. Confronting the Differences
3. Power Struggles
4. Fight or Flight
5. Intractable

Awareness of Differences

At the preconflict level, members become aware that others in the church disagree with them on important matters. Some people have aggressive evangelistic goals for the church while others put more emphasis on discipleship. Some value a structured, formal

---

*Our approach differs from that of Leas on this point. He calls his first two levels of conflict "Problems to Solve" and "Disagreement." Since our definition of conflict includes a power struggle, our first level of conflict "Power Struggles" is the same as his third level "Contest."

worship style while others value an informal, less-structured service. For the awareness of differences to exist, the differences must be significant.

Now members must decide how to respond. They can tell themselves that differences are to be expected in the church and decide to live with it. They will only do this if they see more risk in exposing their differences than in confronting them. People are not likely to expose the fact that they disagree if they think people who are important to them will be displeased and their place in the group will be jeopardized.

At this point, the differing members have not engaged each other on the differences, but they may have discussed them with the pastor or other members they know and trust. These discussions are designed to help the members determine if they are alone in their thinking. In higher levels the purpose of these discussions will be to recruit allies.

If church leaders discover that members are differing over significant issues, they should attempt to get a rational discussion going with those members.

Communication about the issues at this point is very rational, emotions are under control, and those involved are taking full responsibility for their positions. Personalities are not involved, and they are directly confronting just the issues. If they determine that the evidence does not support their conclusion, they are open to modifying their positions.

If church leaders discover that members are differing over significant issues, they should attempt to get a rational discussion going with those members. At this point the members need information that will help them understand the issues more fully. They may be open to alternative points of view that could result in better understanding of themselves, their church, and their faith. This is an important growth opportunity for these members and the church as a whole.

Confronting the Differences

At this second precursor level of conflict members decide to confront the differences they perceive with others in the church. Their goal is to get others to agree with their position.

They begin to form arguments that they think will be persuasive in getting church leadership to see things their way. If they are in conflict with church leaders, they begin thinking of ways to get other members to support them. They are designing strategies that they hope will result in their values and interests prevailing in the church.

The openness to other ideas that we found in level one is missing in level two. The objective now is more about persuading others to agree with them than it is to fully understand the issues. They decide whether new information is right or wrong based on whether it confirms what they already believe. Evidence supporting their position is accepted; evidence refuting their position is rejected.

Communication at level one was characterized by rational, specific descriptions of the problem. At this level people focus more on trends or movements they perceive as either supporting or threatening their positions (Leas 2001c, 19). It becomes harder to get people to make clear connections between evidence and conclusions in their arguments about issues. They don't feel as close to some people in the church as they once did. When they actually engage in discussions with those with whom they differ, it is often difficult to see how their responses match with the point the other person is making.

Whether the two sides will begin to listen to each other depends highly on the amount of trust between the two factions and the amount of trust both sides feel toward church leadership.

We see increasing emotional distancing from those with whom they differ. Some say this distance is being created to prepare for an attack. Before they can feel justified in attacking the opponent, the opponent must be made out to be the enemy.

In addition to emotional distance, the emotional "tide" is rising at level two. This should be the focus of church leaders who are attempting to keep these differences from developing into a power struggle. This is the optimal point for church leaders to have a positive influence. If they can intervene before the power struggle breaks out into the open, it will be easier to get the parties to listen to each other. Once people make their stands on issues public, it is difficult to get them to change.

Whether the two sides will begin to listen to each other depends highly on the amount of trust between the two factions and the amount of trust both sides feel toward church leadership. Leaders must focus on helping all members see that everyone in the church is committed to the same mission or purpose and reassure both parties that leadership can be trusted to protect the parties' respective interests. If that base of trust is established, then perhaps the leader can help the members trust each other.

Muzafer Sherif's research demonstrated the importance of getting people of differing positions to focus on what he called "superordinate goals."* This takes the focus off the differences and places it on the aspects of the community that all members hold in common. In the church setting, leaders can help differing members see the church's mission or vision for the future as a superordinate goal. Ideally, members will direct their individual goals and objectives toward achieving the mission the Lord has for the church.

Note that we are not saying that these members should put aside their individual interests, because that is unlikely. Rather they must see that their individual interests will be achieved at least as well, if not more fully, by focusing on the more all-encompassing goal of the church's mission.

We referred earlier to a church member who said to a pastor, "We don't agree on much, but I trust your heart." Once trust like this has been established, a foundation has been created on which to base a discussion of the issues.

---

*Taken from graduate course in social psychology attended by author and taught by Carolyn Sherif at Pennsylania State University, 1972.

Perhaps an ad hoc committee could be formed to address the issue with representatives of the differing positions asked to serve on the committee. Sherif's research demonstrated conclusively that putting those of differing opinions in the same group to work together works only at levels one and two of the conflict. Once the conflict has broken out into the open, this strategy has less chance of working.

When people at high conflict levels are put together in a group charged with arriving at a mutually acceptable solution, the meeting becomes a new arena in which to wage the conflict. Rather than a productive problem-solving exercise, this often adds fuel to the fire and does not have a positive outcome.

Power Struggles

At this first open conflict level, the differences between members have broken out into win-lose power struggles (Leas 2001c, 20). Uninvolved members begin to notice that people on one side of the conflict are consciously avoiding contact with those on the other side. Of course, this separation only serves to keep the conflict from being resolved, but the emotional tide is now so high that members of opposing groups feel uncomfortable being around each other.

Communication at this level is marked by distortion, innuendo, and extremes. Those outside the conflict are confused by people they considered rational making highly irrational statements.

The power struggle becomes evident as members form alliances to defeat the "enemy." All energies are now directed into winning the battle; discussions are about personalities rather than issues. Strategies are planned to exclude the opposing party from the church's decision-making processes.

Members are not yet at the point of attempting to drive the opposition from the church, which is typical of the fight or flight stage. At this level the parties are still engaging each other as members of the same organization. They believe they will eventually be able to win the battle and those who opposed them will come around.

Those who are attempting to manage the conflict should begin by working with the respective sides separately in an effort to lower the intensity of emotions. Only then will they be able to rationally discuss issues. If emotions are especially high, church leaders may want to seek outside help to deal with the situation. Speed Leas takes the position that outside help is needed in most churches when the conflict actually breaks out into the open.

> *Conflict managers may be able to help opposing parties see that they share similar interests even though they have taken very different positions in the conflict.*

Outside help can be particularly vital if the pastor is one of the parties to the conflict. Once the pastor is identified as a party to the conflict, he or she loses the ability to have significant influence on those who are taking the opposing view. It may be in the pastor's best interest to bring in outside help so that the conflict does not move to the fight or flight level where major segments of the church are working to drive the pastor and his or her allies out of the church.

The conflict manager's primary goal at this level is to encourage the development of a cooperative rather than competitive frame for the discussions and to focus on interests rather than on positions (Ury 1999, 41-42). Conflict managers may be able to help opposing parties see that they share similar interests even though they have taken very different positions in the conflict. Once similar interests are identified, a more cooperative frame can be placed on the discussions.

Fight or Flight

When conflict reaches this level, it is very dangerous to the well-being of the church as a whole, membership and leadership alike. Now the fighting parties are taking the position that there is not enough room in the church for them and the members on the other side of the issue. The focus on what is good for the church as a whole is replaced by what is good only for one's own coalition or subgroup.

Communication is reduced to bitter, hurtful comments intended to drive others out of the church. If by the grace of God there is a positive outcome to the conflict, when it is over, some members will need to ask for forgiveness and repent for some of the things they said and did.

> *The advantage of an outside consultant is that he or she is not automatically viewed as someone who is biased toward the pastor's side of the conflict.*

The pastor and board should not assume that they have the resources necessary to deal with conflict at this level without outside help. Neither should they appoint an individual who leads one of the warring coalitions to head up a task force to look into the problem (Leas 2001c, 22). There is little likelihood that one who has already taken one side or the other will be able to focus on the good of the church. It is more likely such a person will do whatever serves his or her coalition, hoping in the end to drive out the opposition.

If the pastor is a party to such a conflict, it may or may not help to involve higher denominational authorities. Pastors who responded to our survey reported both positive and negative results of such intervention. The advantage of an outside consultant is that he or she is not automatically viewed as someone who is biased toward or against the pastor's side of the conflict.

Intractable

In describing this most intense level of conflict, Speed Leas writes, "An example of this kind of behavior in churches is where members of a church which has dismissed a pastor feel constrained to see that the pastor does not get another church position, and hinder the pastor's search" (22). Parties to the conflict at this level are not just angry, they are out for revenge, hoping to do real harm to those on the other side.

Here the language takes on the characteristics of what Eric Hoffer calls the "true believer." Such a person believes that he or she is fighting for eternal principles of much greater importance than any local issue. The other side is characterized as having evil intents, which can only be responded to by attack. An all-out effort to drive them out of the church is launched.

Those who disagree with the "true believers" are called "evil" and "out to destroy our church." They may even be labeled as "aligned with the forces of Satan." The prognosis is very poor for a successful conclusion to conflict at this level.

FROM THE PASTOR'S DESK . . . *As pastor of a large church, I chair a church board with a diverse group of construction workers, homemakers, university professors, medical doctors, union workers, teachers, lawyers, home-school parents, and so forth, who have every imaginable perspective and expectation for the church.*

Recently some of our youth interns were required to attend a church board meeting for a class at the university, and it was a meeting consisting of a one-hour discussion of one agenda item with motions, amendments, substitute motions, motions for the previous question, and about every possible parliamentary procedure in Robert's Rules of Order. Afterward, one of the wide-eyed interns asked what I thought about all the comments from the fellow on the back row. I explained that I thought he asked some good questions. His arguments perfected the recommendation into a better decision than it would have been without the courteous but spirited discussion. I knew this group of individuals and trusted them to handle the conflict in a positive and constructive way. After the meeting, members whose opinions differed during the discussion lingered together in the hallways and on the parking lot laughing and talking about their golf scores and making points they forgot to bring out in the previous discussion. It was the Body of Christ at its best.

If as the presiding leader I had sensed that the reasoned discussion with emotions under control was getting out of hand and focusing on personalities, if I had discerned that there was a growing lack of love and trust that might undermine the unity of our community, if they started attacking those on the other side of the issue as though they were the "enemy," then it would have been my responsibility to step in to keep the conflict from emerging into a win-lose power struggle.

When conflict is not handled lovingly, it not only is a distraction to Christian believers but also consumes essential resources that should be channeled toward the mission of the church. The world will be more apt to believe that Jesus was sent by God to the earth—not just when we have better evangelistic tools and excellent buildings and inspiring music and seeker-sensitive sermons—the world will believe He is the answer as they see us lovingly problem-solve.

5

EARLY WARNING SIGNALS AND CREATING FIREWALLS

O ver the years school shootings have rocked the United States. These destructive conflicts have created a thirst for information on the warning signs that violence is about to erupt.

As it turns out, in almost every instance there were largely ignored early indications that trouble was brewing. A lot of attention is now being focused on two things: Learning to identify early warning signs and learning how to respond when the warning signs appear.

William Ury, in his book *Getting to Peace*, describes many conflicts where identifying early warning signs were picked up and officials intervened, successfully averting a destructive situation. Church leaders can learn important lessons here about detecting trouble and intervening to forestall a conflict's potentially damaging effects.

Why Is Early Intervention Effective?

Identifying early warning signals of conflict and intervening effectively has two important benefits. The first is that those involved can deal with the conflict when emotions are under control and before it becomes explosive.

Also, dealing with early warning signs often keeps a second wave of conflict from developing. Suppose a church is dealing with fewer and fewer people volunteering for jobs in the church. This could be an early sign that conflict is developing. If church leaders deal with this right away, they may avoid a much nastier conflict over why they didn't act sooner. It's much less tumultuous to deal with a drop in the number of volunteers than with frustration among members over a lack of leadership.

Let's discuss some early warning signals of church conflict and what church leaders can do to create "firewalls" to keep the conflict from destroying their churches.

EARLY WARNING SIGNALS

Early warning signals of potential conflict in churches come in three forms: attitudes, behaviors, and systemic indicators.

Attitudes

Three attitudes that are breeding grounds for conflict are closed-mindedness, authoritarianism, and a win-lose orientation. When these attitudes are found in the church, the seed of conflict has been planted.

Closed-mindedness is probably the attitude of church members that most frequently leads to conflict. A member who suffers from closed-mindedness sees everyone in the church in one of two camps: those who agree with him or her and those who are wrong.

Imagine the response of closed-minded people when a new pastor makes suggestions on changes that should be made to attract new members. The pastor is at first gently informed that things have been done this way for many years. If the pastor persists, he or she is reminded that the people who support the church and pay his or her salary want things to remain the way they are. If the pastor remains convinced that changes should be made, the power struggle likely breaks out into the open and the church is in conflict.

People develop and maintain attitudes because those attitudes serve their interests. When a worship style, version of the Bible, or approach to Bible study provides a sense of security for people, they develop attitudes that will help protect the things that are comfortable for them. People can defend their interests more easily when they are convinced that their way is right and all others are wrong. They begin to build a defensive structure to ward off opposition. They look for Bible verses to support their position. They build alliances with others who agree with them. They read books by authors who agree with their position. In extreme cases, those who dare disagree are seen as attacking the Bible and the church.

When church leaders see extremely closed-minded attitudes developing, they should take this as an early warning sign that conflict is on the way.

Authoritarianism develops when closed-minded people develop a strong desire to control other members. If these people get into positions of power, they not only are not open to change but also are in a position to impose their views on others.

The authoritarian attitude of the pastor is a frequent source of church conflict, especially if the pastor has been at the church for an extended time (10 years or more).

Some pastors become convinced that they know better than anyone else what is right for the church. They resist other views and use their power to entrench their positions. Other pastors become comfortable with a particular way of doing things and then convince themselves that it is the only right way. Still others develop a defensiveness growing out of their own personal insecurity, and they develop an authoritarian attitude to ward off challenges to their positions. The one pastor who indicated that pastors are a source of conflict estimated that half of church conflicts are caused by defensiveness on the pastor's part.

Trouble may begin when new people come into the church with ideas for change they think will help the church grow. The pastor with an authoritarian personality quickly resorts

The cooperative *personality looks for ways to agree with others to build strong relationships.*

to power moves to ward off the attack, and the church finds itself in conflict.

A **win-lose attitude** is the third early warning sign that the church is headed for conflict. People with this attitude see themselves in competition with those around them. Every disagreement is a battle where someone will win and someone else will lose. The *cooperative* personality looks for ways to agree with others to build strong relationships. The *competitive* personality looks for weaknesses in others to use as a way to gain an advantage.

Behaviors

Certain behaviors can signal that conflict may be on the way. When leaders see these behaviors, they should be on the lookout for conflict.

Drop in attendance is one of the earliest indicators of emerging conflict (Leas 2001c, 14). It may mean that those who are frustrated but not heavily invested in the church are leaving. Even more worrisome, however, is that others who are frustrated and heavily invested may be staying to fight. This is why it is important to talk with people who leave the church. Church leaders may discover frustrations they were unaware of and can then take action to address them.

Withholding of financial resources and withdrawal of membership are two other indicators, but they are generally not as early a warning as drop in attendance (14). Withdrawal of membership may not occur until the church conflict is well under way. Church leaders make a mistake if they do not take action until members begin to withdraw their membership. There are almost certainly other early warning signals they are ignoring.

Withdrawal of personal contacts should be taken as an early warning sign of approaching conflict (14). Sometimes the pastor will notice that people who often talked with him or her in the past hardly stop to talk at all anymore or may stop coming to functions they know the pastor will attend. This development should be looked into to see if there is trouble brewing.

While there may be other very understandable reasons for

these changes, such as a revised work schedule, an expression of concern from the pastor may go a long way. If there is a problem, the pastor has taken the initiative to address it.

An increase in complaints is another behavioral indicator that conflict may be on the way (14). Every church has chronic complainers, so the pastor must have his or her hand on the pulse of the church to know when the number and severity of complaints has increased. When members who are usually satisfied begin to complain, church leadership should pay attention.

Deterioration in critical church relationships. Mary was the secretary at the Colonial Hills Community Church. She liked to tell people she had trained two pastors, three youth pastors, and two worship ministers during her 10 years as church secretary. Mark was the fourth youth pastor to come along during her tenure.

Sue, the senior pastor, was starting to get vibes that things were not going well between Mary and Mark. Mark was enormously popular with the young people of the church. He stayed up until all hours of the night with them, visited them at their high schools, and had a wonderful sense of humor.

One day Mary overheard one of the young people saying how refreshing it was to have a youth pastor with a sense of humor. The teenager said she was tired of adults in the church who were sourpusses like Mary. Mary was devastated. She began asking her friends if they thought she was a sourpuss, and of course, her friends told her they didn't think so at all. She told her friends that ever since Mark came as youth pastor, the teens had been referring to her as a sourpuss.

I get tired of the adults in the church sometimes. You all need to lighten up.

One of Mary's friends, Anne, was the mother of two teens in the group. Anne took her daughter Kim aside one day.

"Kim, how are things going in the teen group?"

"Oh, great, Mom. I think Mark is awesome."

"What makes him so great?"

"He's just like us. He has a great sense of humor. He has us laughing most of the time."

"I hope he gets serious sometimes."

"Mom," Kim replied with an obvious tone of exasperation in her voice, "he's a pastor. That's what pastors do. What do you think, he has to be serious all the time? I get tired of the adults in the church sometimes. You all need to lighten up. Especially Mary. She's a real grouch."

Anne was barely able to restrain her anger at hearing her friend described that way. "Who told you Mary was a grouch?"

Now Kim is really getting irritated. She answers with anger rising in her voice.

"You see, Mom, that's exactly what I mean. You adults are always trying to crack down on somebody. Lighten up!"

Anne is not used to Kim talking to her that way. She is convinced that the things Kim is saying must have come from Mark.

Meanwhile, Mark is beginning to resent Mary talking to him as though she were his boss. He realizes he had a lot to learn, but he figured that once he began to learn his way around she would recognize him as a professional and not tell him what to do so much. Unfortunately, he had seen no sign of that, and it was really beginning to get to him.

In fact, Mark was being very professional about his relationship with Mary. He had not said a word about her to the teens and certainly did not refer to her as a sourpuss. He had heard several of the teens talk about her that way, however. One night when he heard them talking that way, he confronted them.

"Hey, you guys, that's no way to talk about Mary."

"Aw, come on, Mark," said Brian. "Mary could turn milk sour just by looking at it. I'll bet she wakes up with a frown from ear to ear every morning. I can just hear her now. 'There go those teenagers again, acting like life was fun or something.'"

Jennifer chimed in her support, imitating Mary's high-pitched voice perfectly. "You kids are beginning to get on my nerves." The whole group laughed.

Mark decided then that he was going to gear an upcoming devotional to a discussion about being loving in relationships. He also knew he was going to have to talk with Sue about his relationship with Mary because right now he did not feel very loving toward her himself.

When Pastor Sue learns that this conflict is developing, hopefully she will realize that the conflict between Mark and Mary is only one aspect of it. It has the potential to spin off into conflicts between teens and parents as well as between Mark and parents. If she approaches it as only between Mary and Mark, she will miss early warning signs of other conflicts that are developing.

One pastor who filled out our survey wrote about problems that developed between the church's secretary and the children's pastor in his church. These people in critical positions could begin to build alliances around them. Before you know it, you have warring camps in opposition to each other.

A pastor could take the approach that these two adults should be able to work this out for themselves. This pastor, however, took the deterioration as an early warning signal and took the initiative. He talked to each of them separately to express his concern. He asked that they let him know if there was some way he could help them address their differences. Fortunately, the situation appeared to be improving.

Sometimes church members and staff members—particularly those in important positions—have **poor communication skills in handling differences with others.** If this is the case, it is an early warning signal that conflict is likely to break out in the areas where they serve.

While the pastor may be able to make a change in the case of the staff member, it would not be so easy with a church member in an elected position. One of the difficulties with volunteer organizations is that there may not be anyone else who can fill the position the person holds. In that case, church leadership must be continually alert for potential conflict coming from those areas. This is not an enviable position for any church leader.

Provoking incidents should always be considered an early warning of potential conflict. In the most extreme cases, this would include threatening remarks or charges that are made against others in the church. These comments should never be passed off lightly or assumed to be nothing but talk.

One pastor who completed our survey wrote about a person in the church having a dream about an older member of the church. In her dream this older man had committed a serious crime. She told her granddaughter, who was a member of the church's teen group, that she should stay away from that man because he had committed a serious crime. The girl then told her youth pastor what her grandmother had said.

Unfortunately, this situation did not turn out well. In the end the youth pastor had to leave the church, and the incident turned out badly for the teen and her family. When incidents like this occur, the pastor should assume that it would take a miracle to keep conflict from erupting. These sorts of incidents have the potential of doing great damage to churches, to the careers of pastors, and to the lives of the people in the church.

Pastors and church members alike must be held accountable for their words, particularly when they are threatening or accusatory in nature. Unless these members are confronted in love about this type of talk, it can become a cancer that is destructive to Christian community in the church.

Systemic Indicators

Sometimes there are signs in the system itself that conflict is on the way.

One of these is the **tendency for the relationships between people in the church to be superficial.** The communication systems in some churches tell members to always put on a happy face. People tend to keep their problems and frustrations to themselves because of unspoken messages to say something positive or say nothing at all. If these frustrations build to an explosion, the church will have a big problem that will probably necessitate outside help.

A second sign of impending problems in the system is that **church leaders are unable or unwilling to recognize problems**

(Leas 2001c, 26). Pastors and lay leaders often say they are the last to know what is going on in the church. This happens sometimes because members sense—rightly or wrongly—that leadership doesn't really want to hear about problems. Again, frustrations within the membership build.

In some cases, people in leadership positions are really not interested in knowing the frustrations members have with what is happening at the church. In either case, the frustrated members are without a healthy means of addressing their differences.

A third systemic factor is the existence of a **competitive goal structure in the church** (Johnson and Johnson 1982, 251). Pastors, like other leaders, should be careful not to set up competitive reward systems in the church that lead people to believe that the only way they can succeed is if someone else fails. Some kinds of competition in a church are healthy, but members should never feel that they must compete with others for the approval of the pastor or other leaders.

People are more attracted by those who agree with them than by those who disagree.

Another system signal occurs **when members form power alliances rather than directly address their differences** (Leas 2001d, 17). People are more attracted by those who agree with them than by those who disagree. Therefore, when a difference of opinion develops, they avoid the person who disagrees, forming coalitions with people who share their opinion, rather than directly addressing their differences. Warring camps are formed, frustrations increase, and differences go unaddressed.

CREATING FIREWALLS

Firewalls are built into computer systems to keep viruses and other unwanted intrusions out of the system. In the same way, churches can build "firewalls" into the church's communication system to help keep conflict from doing serious damage (Gulbranson 1998).

Firewalls can serve two important purposes in the church. First, they can keep some frustrations from developing by dealing with situations before conflict breaks out. Second, they provide a means of dealing early on with those frustrations that do develop while they are still manageable.

There are four important strategies pastors can take to construct firewalls in the congregation.

1. Openly acknowledge that conflict is expected and can be an avenue for growth.
2. Develop a reputation for fair and equitable decisions.
3. Develop an early alert system.
4. Establish a Community Development Team.

Openly acknowledge that conflict is expected and an avenue for growth. When people realize that conflict is a normal part of any church life, they are more likely to talk about the conflicts they observe. Church members are more inclined to express their opinions when they realize that having people of differing opinions is a strength rather than a weakness. The more ideas the church has to draw from on how to make the church grow, the better off it will be.

People with differing points of view will be watching to see if their ideas are just dropped or are taken seriously. If the pastor listens politely, smiles, nods, and then does what he or she was planning to do all along, members get cynical and frustrated. When differences of opinion are expressed, it is very important that church leadership welcomes and seriously considers all suggestions.

Develop a reputation for fair and equitable decisions. Church members must perceive that when they express their frustrations, they get a fair hearing followed by a process that treats all members fairly (Ury 1999, 172). The church is not immune to situations in which powerful families are given preferential treatment.

The pastor must make sure that all constituencies in the church are listened to carefully (Pneuman 2001, 53) and responded to fairly. This allows construction of another firewall that keeps conflict from having its potentially destructive effects on the development of Christian community.

This is particularly important with regard to distributing the church's resources. These resources could be finances, the pastor's time and energies, physical space, or materials. The process by which those resources are allocated throughout the church should demonstrate that all parties have equal representation and consideration.

Develop an early alert system. Training church members to identify the warning signals of impending conflict will create an early alert system to spot "smoldering embers" before they erupt into flames. The people who are closest to frustrated members will be the first to see the early warning signs and are the ideal ones to alert church leadership that trouble may be brewing (Ury 1999, 131).

To build these firewalls, the pastor must take three actions:

1. Convince all members that it is important for everyone to be on the alert for early warning signs.
2. Train members to identify early warning signs.
3. Develop response strategies to be implemented when early warning signs are detected.

Church members should have training to learn to manage differences before the differences become power struggles. This training builds firewalls throughout the church that prevent minor conflicts from developing into big problems.

As churches grow, the church staff cannot be personally involved in resolving all conflicts that develop. As the church organization becomes more complex, it will need a more highly developed system of responding to conflict. Developing an early alert system can provide such a firewall.

Establish a community development team. Universities and businesses are increasingly seeing the need to establish teams to provide someone for people to contact when they observe conflict developing. Many organizations find this is a very effective strategy for reducing the number and severity of conflicts.

This team can make an important contribution by providing anonymity for members who need to address differences with each other. Obviously, people chosen for this responsibility must have proven themselves as spiritually mature, good problem solvers, and committed to hold information in the strictest confidence.

FROM THE PASTOR'S DESK . . . *My father-in-law, Dr. Hardy C. Powers, was a gifted leader who anticipated conflict before it was apparent in the family or the church. He once said to my wife, Jeannie, after a pastor had walked away, reflecting on the advice he had shared, "That pastor is a good and godly man, but he lacks cat whiskers." He explained that the whiskers on a cat permit this animal to sense and detect objects before it runs into a brick wall. But he said this man runs full speed into a closed door, and when his nose is bleeding and his eye is black and swollen, he says, "This is a door."*

Good leaders realize when the warning signs of conflict and frustration are present and anticipate them before someone is hurt and becomes a casualty.

Preventive work includes preaching and teaching the biblical principles of how to care for, pray for, and listen to one another. Modeling openness and loving people provides the bridge for our people to give us feedback. The larger the church grows, the more essential it is that senior pastors have staff members who recognize the indicators of conflict.

When I have led the church I pastor through significant change, open forums have provided a time for questions, even anonymously submitted on 4" x 6" cards, so that the misunderstandings, misinformation, and rumors can be addressed to preclude divisive conflict.

As a pastor I have learned that it is important to be a good listener and be open-minded to the views of all members. Sometimes this will mean taking the leaders of both sides of an issue to lunch to let them know you want to carefully listen to their positions. Conflict will be reduced if those involved know you do not have a bias toward either side and they have the opportunity to feel your spirit and trust your heart.

6

THE ROLES
PEOPLE PLAY

There's a war raging in the Mars Hill Church that provides a good example of the family-member-types of roles individuals fall into during church conflict.

During the week, the Mars Hill facility is used as a day school and is run by Marsha, a member of the church. Marsha is continually criticized by the church's Sunday School teachers because the Sunday School classrooms are in terrible disarray almost every Sunday morning. The Sunday School teachers say the day school teachers act like they're the only ones using the classrooms. Materials are left out on the tables, equipment is not put away, and Sunday School supplies are used by the school and not replaced. The Sunday School teachers claim it takes at least a half hour on Sunday mornings to get their rooms ready for class.

Allen, the Sunday School director, is extremely frustrated and feels the church's day school should be closed if the situation is not remedied. He points out that the day school has not been instrumental in bringing new people into the church in its 10-year existence—which was the primary reason the school was started. The school is barely breaking even financially and he feels the resources being poured into the school could be used more effectively in other efforts.

Mike, the youth and children's pastor, feels caught in the middle between Allen and Marsha. The senior pastor, Wayne, has asked Mike for his recommendations but is beginning to recognize that Mike generally parrots Marsha's argument that the school is a ministry to children who would not get religious instruction were it not for the school. Wayne realizes that Mike doesn't seem to recognize the legitimacy of the concerns raised by Allen and the Sunday School teachers.

One morning Allen called Pastor Wayne and informed him that three of the Sunday School teachers were going to resign if the situation wasn't resolved. He said he had talked to Marsha about it several times and the last time she suggested that the Sunday School teachers were exaggerating about the condition of the classrooms on Sunday mornings.

When Pastor Wayne suggested that he would ask Mike to meet with Allen and Marsha to get the issue resolved, Allen told him that Marsha had Mike wrapped around her little finger. He requested that the matter be put on the agenda of the next board meeting; it was time for the church to decide if it wanted a Sunday School program or a day school. Allen's belief was that if the board voted to keep the day school, then many of the Sunday School teachers would tender their resignations.

When the discussion of what to do about the school came up in the next board meeting, the arguments the pastor heard more than any others were Marsha's arguments for keeping the school open, even though she wasn't in the room. He tried to support Allen's concerns, particularly the idea of thinking of other ways to bring new people into the church, but his efforts had little effect on the outcome of the discussion. While some board members agreed with Pastor Wayne, most said nothing. It was obvious that the subject of doing something about the day school was not up for discussion.

Tom, one of the board members, spoke up. "Pastor, I don't think this board has ever really considered what the real mission of our church is. Why are we here? What are we trying to accomplish? If we don't know what our mission is, how will we know if we're accomplishing it?" Again, there was no response. The issue was dead.

THE CHURCH AS A FAMILY

When striving to understand what is happening during a church conflict of this kind, it is helpful to think of the participants as members of a family. For the balance of this chapter we will use this approach to help us understand the difficulty that has arisen in the Mars Hill Church.*

Principal Players

You will generally find that there are no more than five principal players in a church conflict (Halverstadt 1991, 84). If you are having difficulty identifying the principal players, it might help to first identify the social or political groups in the church. All organizations, including churches, are organized into social or political groups. Some may be organized by age, such as senior citizens or parents of teenagers. Other groups may be more political in nature.

> *Conflicts are about power, and one of the first things those involved in power struggles do is attempt to build a coalition of support.*

Conflicts are about power, and one of the first things those involved in power struggles do is attempt to build a coalition of support. The principal players have likely recruited a group of people for a power base from which to wage the conflict. Perhaps there is a group lobbying for a particular worship style or a new church building. Often the major players in a church conflict are people who represent groups such as these. Once you identify the group, it is then easier to determine the identity of the group's leaders.

If you identify the social subgroups or political segments in the community, those who generally represent or speak for these

---

*Cosgrove and Hatfield, in their book *Church Conflict: The Hidden Systems Behind the Fights,* use this family systems approach to help us understand the roles people play in church conflicts. Their approach also helps us know how to work toward making conflict a positive aspect of church growth.

groups should be considered possible principal players to the conflict.

Identifying the principal players might sound easy to do, but sometimes it isn't, particularly in church conflicts. People are often not open about the fact that they are at odds with others in the church. At times there seems to be an unwritten rule that Christians aren't supposed to disagree. Therefore, some members try to cover up their conflicts with a masquerade of being on good terms with everyone.

At other times the principal players are hard to identify because some of the parties are fighting unfairly. To cover up they put on the pretense that they would never fight with someone in the church and, if asked, would deny it.

Therefore, either because Christians are not supposed to fight or because some of the parties are fighting unfairly, it may be hard to identify the principal parties to the church conflict.

Parents and Children

Once you have identified the principal players in the conflict, the next step is to identify the roles played by each of the major and minor participants, and at this point the family metaphor comes more fully into play. The *family structure* of a church is the way the church members informally decide who has the power to influence the church's decisions.

Often this informal family structure will be more powerful than the church's formal board and committee structure (Cosgrove and Hatfield 1994, 24). Frequently the principal players in the conflict will take on the roles of parents in the church family. When the informal parents of the family exercise their authority, they do not have to convince others to follow their lead; they do not have to win elections to gain their official positions. Their authority is just accepted because of their role as parent (61-62).

People who wield this authority are not labeled as parents because they are more mature than others in the church or because the pastor has decided they should be parents. They are parents because others in the church follow their lead. In the Mars Hill

Church, Marsha is clearly a parent in the church's informal family structure. Even though she has no position on the church board, board members are following her lead with regard to the church's school. When Pastor Wayne listened to the discussion in the church board meeting, it was as though Marsha was present in the meeting. It became clear that a significant number of church board members were "children" whose "parent" was Marsha.

As in the parent role, those who play the *child role* in the system are not necessarily called that because of their maturity level or their willingness to accept responsibility. They are children because they have chosen to follow the lead of the parent. They have decided to do whatever it is their parent suggests they do. Mike handles much responsibility as the church's youth and children's pastor; however, he is a child in the church system because he follows Marsha's lead.

Church members often take roles in church similar to those they took in their families of origin. If an individual tended to accept the influence of a strong, authoritative person in his or her natural family, that person may find it very difficult to counter a strong, authoritative "parent" in the church. Even a pastor may have a hard time standing up to an authoritative layperson on the board who plays the role of parent. In this case, the layperson is the real power in the church. In an ideal situation, however, the pastor is a parent in the church's family structure.

Parents within the same family-type structure are not necessarily in conflict with one another. They can and often do defer to each other by mutually agreeing to divide up responsibility in the church. One church parent assembles a family subgroup around him or her for organizing evangelistic efforts while another parent assembles a different family subgroup for taking care of the church's discipling activities.

This can cause increasing interdependence, however, and the areas of responsibility can sometimes overlap, causing more conflict (Ury 1999, 99-100). These situations can be effectively negotiated as long as there is an *open boundary* between the parents. Parents must negotiate based on areas of expertise rather than the desire to exercise power. "Parents" with *rigid boundaries* and negative uses of power will produce a church with a great deal of harmful conflict.

The parental role is not determined by the affection the parent has for others or by the affection others have for the parent. The parental role is determined by the informal authority the parent has over others in the system.

The parental child. Sometimes the pastor wants members of his or her pastoral staff to behave more as a *parental child,* a role similar to that of older siblings in a literal family. Staff members who play this role willingly accept the pastor's authority, but others in the church look to them for leadership. They are given considerable latitude in making decisions in their given areas, but everyone recognizes that the pastor is the final authority. If the pastor expects the staff member to act like a parental child while the staff member chooses to take the "child" role, there will be problems in the relationship. The pastor will think the staff member is not exerting leadership while the staff member will feel the pastor is not exerting appropriate leadership.

The independent child. Just as an *independent child* in a natural family resists obedience to either parent, independent children in church families do not follow the lead of any parent in the church. On one hand, the independent child can be the voice of reason in calling for calm discussion rather than following the lead of either parent. On the other hand, he or she can cause real trouble by refusing to cooperate with anyone. Some pastors and lay leaders find it difficult to work with independent children because they do not automatically follow the lead of those in authority or in parent roles.

It is clear from Tom's contribution to the discussion in the board meeting that he plays the role of the independent child in the Mars Hill Church. He does not follow the lead of either the pastor or Marsha. He calls for examining the issue from the perspective of the church's mission and could end up supporting either side.

Boundaries

Once the roles of those involved in the conflict are identified, it is time to analyze the nature of the boundaries between the players. The fact that a layperson operates in a parent role does not mean that he or she is in conflict with the pastor. Looking at the boundary between the "parents" will help determine whether they are in conflict and what that conflict is like.

In examining the boundary, look for two things. One is the means the parties use in their attempts to influence each other. The second is the quality of the communication that flows across the boundary.

An **open boundary** means that there is a reasonable opportunity for the two parties to have open, meaningful communication. Even though there is conflict, the parties are attempting to influence each other with reason and appeal to facts. This is a sign that the parties are willing to develop a good working relationship to negotiate conflicts. However, if one of the parties becomes defensive, the boundary can quickly change and so does the nature of the conflict.

Each party's only interest is in overpowering or driving out the opponent.

If, at the onset of the conflict however, there is a *rigid,* **closed boundary,** this indicates that the communication is poor. There is little or no open, honest communication, and the possibility of the parties working out a conflict between themselves is not good.

In the Mars Hill conflict there is a rigid boundary between Marsha the day school director and Allen the Sunday School director. There is no reasonable discussion of the issues on which to build an agreement. Each party's only interest is in overpowering or driving out the opponent.

A third type of boundary, the **diffuse boundary,** exists when one person is too close to another person and the parties have difficulty acting independently. A diffuse boundary exists between Mike, the youth and children's pastor, and Marsha. There is no clear and open discussion on the issues of the day school between the two of them. They tend to act so much in concert with each other that neither of them has an independent position.

There can also be combinations of these boundary types. A **disputed boundary** is when one party attempts to communicate as parent to parent, but the other does not respond from the parent role. A disputed boundary exists between Pastor Wayne and Mike. Pastor Wayne attempts to discuss issues with Mike as two respectful parents do, but Mike responds, not as a parent to people in the church, but rather from the position of Marsha's child. The result is lack of clear and open messages flowing between Mike and the pastor. This makes addressing the issue very difficult.

In the Mars Hill conflict those who look to Marsha as the parent in the church family predominate the membership of the church board—including Mike. This places Pastor Wayne in a particularly vulnerable situation. Few board members wish to stand up to Marsha, the dominating parent, demonstrating how the informal family system can be more powerful than the formal organizational system. The pastor is now in the unenviable position of someone else in the family structure having greater influence than he does regarding what to do about the school. If Marsha is "parent" to those board members only on the day school issue, that is one thing. If she is parent on all issues, Pastor Wayne is in an untenable position. She basically controls the "family" and thus the church.

Bystanders

Both Hugh Halverstadt and William Ury give considerable attention to those in the communication system who are not directly involved in the conflict. Halverstadt refers to these people as bystanders while Ury calls them "the third side." Halverstadt writes that

a bystander in a church conflict is a party whose interests—purposes, needs, desires, or responsibilities—are related to the impact of a conflict's resolution on the community or church entity housing it. Bystanders are more invested in how principals resolve their differences than in what principals' resolutions may be. Bystanders are like parties in a fishing boat in which the principals get into a fight. Their primary concern is that the principals' behaviors not sink the boat. (1991, 47)

Ury refers to the third side as "the emergent will of the community" (1999, 14). That will comes to the forefront when these bystanders let it be known to those in conflict that they will not stand idly by and allow the fighting to destroy their community. They are the physical representation of the concern for the common good. This good is of

If the bystanders do nothing, it is very possible that a conflict will destroy or do long-term damage to a church.

greater importance to them than any of the issues causing conflict.

This is not to say that these bystanders will act. We have seen examples in our society of people standing by and watching an innocent person brutally attacked in a public setting. At times the third side is silent, confirming the statement credited to Edmund Burke that "all that is necessary for evil to prosper is for good men to do nothing." If, in fact, the bystanders do nothing, it is very possible that a conflict will destroy or do long-term damage to a church.

However, there is obviously real danger in getting bystanders involved in a church fight. It may serve no purpose but to widen the conflict to a larger portion of the church. The conflict manager will need to carefully orient the bystanders to their important role if this is to be avoided. Properly oriented bystanders can play a critical role in making the conflict a positive, rather than negative, influence in the church.

There is a second risk of using bystanders. The parties to the conflict may get the bystanders to "resolve" the conflict. This eliminates the need for the involved parties to really resolve the conflict between themselves (Halverstadt 1991, 49). When that happens, the conflict manager can be assured that a short-term solution to the conflict has been achieved, and when that happens the conflict is almost certain to erupt again.

One of most important roles bystanders can play in their efforts to protect the common good in the midst of the conflict is to work for a win-win solution. Seldom do all parties come into a church conflict with equal power. Therefore, the bystanders can help balance out the power so that the conflict is addressed by parties of equal strength. "Individually, people may not prove very influential, but collectively they are potentially more powerful than any two conflicting parties. Organizing themselves into a coalition, bystanders can balance the power between the parties and protect the weaker one" (Ury 1999, 15).

When they do this, the bystanders can insist that the interests of all parties are represented. They can arrive at a successful conclusion to the conflict without the powerful parties "steamrolling" over the weaker members. The Bible frequently emphasizes the need for the church to look out for those who are the weaker members of the community. This should be a characteristic means of resolving church conflicts, which distinguishes us from those outside the church.

FROM THE PASTOR'S DESK . . . This chapter contains information that is particularly practical and helpful to church leaders who are looking for insights and useful tools to analyze conflict in the church. Conflicts can be grounded in turf battles, control issues, or gifts of the people involved and the component of the church's mission that the individual is passionate about.

In the case of the Mars Hill Church, Allen made a mistake in creating a win-lose outcome by giving the board an ultimatum. However, it is helpful to raise questions regarding the real mission of the church and determine which ministries will help accomplish this mission. This mission focus is crucial in budget planning, programming decisions, and stewardship of space and staff resources. Making decisions from the perspective of the church's main mission helps to remove the strong personality tendencies to control and influence behind the scenes.

Such conflicts can be assessed by identifying the roles people play in the conflict and by determining if change can occur in the existing system or if the structure or policies have to be changed to make the mission the priority rather than the opinions of one strong personality or family.

7

THE CHURCH AS A COMMUNICATION SYSTEM

The *systems theory* provides a powerful way to grasp a better understanding of why and how conflict occurs in churches. Rather than looking at churches as collections of individuals, the systems approach suggests that we look at individuals in the church as part of a network. We know that not all networks are the same. They differ in important ways that help us understand why the people in a particular network behave the way they do, which can help church leaders analyze their churches as communication systems. This knowledge can help leaders prevent harmful conflict in the first place or provide helpful strategies for effectively handling conflict when it does occur.

Systems theory teaches us the following basic concepts about conflict in the church.

1. Churches are systems with interconnected parts. Each part of a system is in some way related to every other part. To some degree, the whole system is affected when anything—good or bad—happens to one part of the system. There is no such thing as two members having a private battle that does not involve the church as a whole. The impact may be small for some members, but everyone is affected.

No one person can do everything that needs to be done. We have to depend on each other to fulfill the mission to which the Lord has called the church. When we are dependent on other people, what happens to them affects us. Therefore we are in some way interconnected with every other person who is a part of our church.

2. The closer the conflict is to the center of the church, the greater the impact on the church as a whole. If a conflict breaks out between two members who are only marginally involved, the impact on the church as a whole will be slight. If the conflict is between the pastor and members of the board, however, the conflict has the potential of tearing the church apart. From a more positive perspective, however, a conflict between the pastor and members of the church board can produce positive, long-lasting change in the church. It all depends on how the conflict is handled. The important point is that conflict at the central part of a system has significant impact on the whole system.

3. All systems serve some purpose, whether or not the people in the system know what that purpose is. Every human system is serving some purpose, and it is important for people in that system to know what that purpose is. Perhaps a church is holding a neighborhood together just by being where it is, and the members are not even aware of it. Perhaps the only purpose being served by a particular church is keeping the people who are in power in their positions. Whatever the purpose is, all systems achieve a purpose of some kind. People should know what purpose their church is serving and then ask themselves, "Is this the purpose God has for this church, at this time, in this place?"

Conflict often breaks out in church when certain members are unhappy with the church's purpose.

Conflict often breaks out in church when certain members are unhappy with the church's purpose. If the church is caring for the comfortable and avoiding the needy, members with a heart for missions will not be content. If members who think the purpose of the church is to promote middle-class American values see shabbily dressed people welcomed into the church, there will be trouble.

Many churches are in conflict over worship styles. Some church members see the purpose of the church as keeping alive old values and traditions while others see this purpose being achieved, but no new people coming into the church. They want to change the purpose.

A pastor can help prevent serious conflicts in a church by leading the members through the process of answering the following questions.

- What purpose is our church actually serving right now, and how do we know?
- What purpose *should* our church serve (1) at this time, (2) with these members, (3) in this location? (This would be an excellent time to examine the mission statement as well as the objectives flowing out of that statement.)
- If our church is not serving the purpose it should be serving, what must we do to make that happen?
- Are we willing to make the changes, perhaps sacrifices, necessary to make that happen?

Such questions could indeed set off conflict in the church, but conflict may be necessary for growth. Change hurts. But if handled well, changes can result in significant growth for the church, its people, and its pastor.

4. Systems achieve their purposes by giving balance and order to the work of the church. The basic function of a communication system is to provide structure so that people in the system can work together in harmony to achieve their purpose. Individuals can coordinate their efforts by forming a network that allows them to share information about the work they are doing in the system. Policies and procedures are established that help ensure consistency from one part of the network to another. The more people share information about their work with others in the network, the more orderly and balanced the work will be.

5. Systems have "rules" that govern how people communicate in the network. Sometimes these rules are formally written out in policy manuals or handbooks. In other cases these rules are unwritten but people abide by them just the same.

As indicated earlier, churches often observe the unwritten rule that Christians shouldn't fight. This doesn't mean there is no conflict; it simply means that the conflict will be handled covertly rather than out in the open where it could be dealt with more effectively.

6. Almost all systems are made up of a collection of smaller groups or cliques. Identifying these smaller groups is a helpful way to identify the lay leaders in the church. Generally, lay leaders have assumed leadership roles in one of these smaller parts of the communication network. These leaders can play critical roles in a church conflict because either they are in the heat of the conflict or they play an integral role in bringing the conflict to a successful resolution.

7. The whole is greater than the sum of its parts. When people form groups, the dynamics of the group create an identity for the group that cannot be totally explained by looking at the individual members.

CONFLICT AND THE CHURCH COMMUNICATION SYSTEM

Discussing the church as a system does not indicate lack of interest in people as individuals. Rather, studying churches in this way helps us understand individual people better (Halverstadt 1991, 61). The systems perspective also helps us understand how conflict can have a beneficial effect on churches. Parsons and Leas have observed that a church's success can often result in its eventual decline if the church is stuck in a particular way of doing things. Members mistakenly assume that what has been good for the church up to this point will always be good for it, and they lose the creativity and originality that resulted in success in the first place (2001, 62).

The strategies that grew the church from 50 to 100 members will most likely not be the best strategy for growing it from 100 to

200 members. When the environment in which a system exists changes, the system must adjust if it is going to continue to achieve its purpose.

Conflict often challenges the church system to explore new avenues in carrying out its mission and innovative ways to use its resources as efficiently as possible.

That is why Whetten and Cameron observe, "Conflict is the lifeblood of vibrant, progressive, stimulating organizations. It sparks creativity, stimulates innovation and encourages personal improvement" (1998, 321). When conflict blocks the path a system has used for a long time to achieve its purpose, it forces the system to seek out new paths.

Unfortunately, conflict also has the potential of impeding the system's most effective path to achieving its purpose. Pastors and church leaders who ignore conflict do so at their own peril (321). Unresolved conflict may force the system into choosing a path that makes ineffective use of its resources, and people who have significant contributions to make to the church's mission are excluded. The church's ability to meet the needs of the people it is serving will be hampered, causing the church to enter a state of decline.

RULES THAT GOVERN CHURCH SYSTEMS

There are both formal and informal rules about how things should be done in the church. Formal rules can be found in church policy manuals or church board minutes but are generally not as important in understanding how conflict is dealt with in the church as are the informal rules (Halverstadt 1991, 62). A male pastor who is unaware of an informal rule that while women in the church may hug each other, men do not hug the women, can get in big trouble in little time. It doesn't matter that the "rule" is not in writing.

Two types of informal rules make it difficult to deal with conflict in the church: *enmeshment* and *avoidance* (Halverstadt 1991, 62-63). "Enmeshment is a form of empathy without clear borders differentiating 'self' from 'others.' When two persons are enmeshed with each other, they feel each other's feelings as their own. Those who tend toward enmeshment also feel (or imagine they feel) the emotions of others around them and often confuse those emotions with their own" (Cosgrove and Hatfield 1994, 39). When church members have such close emotional ties with each other, it is

When church members have such close emotional ties with each other, it is too risky and hurtful to deal with conflict.

too risky and hurtful to deal with conflict. They fear that the hurt others feel will also hurt them, so they act as though the conflict doesn't exist.

Halverstadt gives the following examples of informal rules of enmeshment, which often exist in churches.

- Christians always take care of others.
- If you can't say something nice, don't say anything.
- Read others' minds rather than know your own.
- Caring Christians don't hurt others' feelings.
- Being kind is more Christian than being honest (1991, 63).

While rules of enmeshment result from too much emotional involvement, rules of *avoidance* result from too little involvement. In this situation, there is such emotional distance between people that they have too little invested in the well-being of others. In their estimation, the risks of engaging in conflict are far greater than the possible benefits. This is often the result of hurtful previous conflicts, and they want to do everything possible to avoid a similar experience.

Halverstadt gives us the following examples of informal avoidance rules.

- Don't bring up things that anger others.
- Deny or discount your own feelings around others.
- Talk in generalities, not specifics.
- Talk only about noncontroversial things like the weather.
- State your own opinions indirectly as hearsay or as "people are saying" (63).

When rules of enmeshment or avoidance are the "laws" that tend to dominate the church's communication system, conflict will not be directly addressed. The unmanaged conflict will continue to damage the church's ability to accomplish its purpose.

Fortunately, there are *constructive informal* rules that can help a church make conflict a positive force. These rules encourage openness that allows the conflict to emerge so members can confront it head-on. These rules are conducive to a high level of trust in the community that allows people to take risks and are essential for healthy communication systems. Old ways of doing things can be challenged, and the church can grow.

Halverstadt provides the following examples of constructive informal rules for dealing with church conflict.

- Be real. Exercise self-control when interacting with others.
- No one here is perfect. Mistakes are human and forgivable.
- No one here is superior or inferior. Everyone is valuable.
- When differences arise, there will be no labeling and no personal attacks.
- Honesty is the best policy.
- Speak for and be yourself.
- No personalizing of issues. Address behaviors, not persons.
- Conflicts are problems to be solved, not contests to be won (65).

POWER

Power, at its simplest, can be defined as the ability to influence others according to the desires of the person exerting the influence. When trying to understand and successfully resolve a church conflict, it is of paramount importance to understand how power is operating in the church communication system. Paul Tillich writes that "every encounter, whether friendly or hostile, whether benevolent or indifferent, is in some way, unconsciously or consciously, a struggle of power with power" (1954, 81).

The discussion of power in scholarly and popular literature tends to have a negative moral tone to it, as though the use of power is a "dirty fighting" technique in church conflicts. The use of power is neither positive nor negative in and of itself, but considering the kind of power used and the purpose for which it is used sets its moral tone. As Halverstadt puts it, "Power is a moral good when it is exercised assertively in accountable, straightforward, and respectful ways with others" (1991, 78).

One reason for a widely held negative view of power in organizations stems from the fact that conflicting members seldom have equal power. When one person has more power than another, we expect the more powerful person to use that power to overwhelm the opposition.

Another reason for the negative view of power is that we believe that not only does power play a critical role in church conflicts, but also one person or party to the conflict only gets power at the expense of others. When you add to this that the accumulation of power in organizations can be intoxicating to some people, these individuals appear to be on a continual drive to control the organization and the lives of those in it.

Those on a power "high" do not seem to understand how threatening it is to others to have more and more of the power in the organization controlled by a person or group with whom they are in conflict. When those who feel threatened decide that the powerful are shutting them out of reasonable control over their own welfare while at the same time their own interests are served by staying in the church, that church is in for a very harmful conflict.

Kinds of Power

In determining the role of power in a church conflict, it is helpful to know the kind of power used.

Reward power is used when those who have control over things or positions that people in the church value use them to influence others. We touched on this earlier in our discussion of sources of church conflict when members perceive that those who agree with the pastor are rewarded with important posts on the church board or other influential positions. Members of the congregation also use reward power over the pastor when they attempt to influence the pastor's decisions with the promise of supporting him or her in the next congregational vote on pastoral renewal.

Coercive power is the flip side of reward power in that it threatens to punish the other if the attempts at influence are rejected. Earlier we cited the example a pastor gave of a music group that formed in his church consisting of several lay leaders. The group was being invited to participate in the Sunday worship services of other churches in their community, necessitating their absence from Sunday morning services at their own church. When the pastor suggested they limit the number of services they would miss or give up their leadership positions in the church, they began to work toward the pastor's removal. They were exercising coercive power by trying to punish the pastor for not supporting what they wanted to do.

A lay leader may attempt to use his or her connections with denominational leaders to influence the pastor.

Pastors or other church members sometimes use **referent power** when they attempt to influence others by emphasizing their connections in networks that are important to the church. For example, a lay leader may attempt to use his or her connections with denominational leaders to influence the pastor. Similarly, pastors can get considerable referent power when it becomes apparent to the membership that the pastor has the ear of denominational hierarchy.

Expert power is one of the most positive ways to influence others in the church in that it is a result of a person's knowledge or information that is critical to the church's ability to successfully fulfill its mission. Whereas the other kinds of power are not based on any resource that is necessarily of any benefit to the church, expert power gives influence to people who genuinely have the ability to help the church fulfill its purpose. Examples of people with expert power are those who are gifted teachers who can contribute significantly to the church's discipleship program or those

When the allocation of power is closely tied to the accomplishment of the church's mission, the use of power is more likely to have a positive effect on resolving church conflicts.

with gifts that enable them to minister to wounded church members and help them deal with the deep hurts of their lives.

When the allocation of power is closely tied to the accomplishment of the church's mission, the use of power is more likely to have a positive effect on resolving church conflicts. When the power base is more political in nature and not of any real benefit to the church's mission, church conflicts tend to be resolved more for the benefit of those exerting the power than for the well-being of the church.

Conflict managers should ask themselves the following questions about the role of power in the church's system:

- What type of power is being used and by whom?
- Toward what end is the power being exerted and will it advance the church's mission?
- What is the balance of power in the church? The manager's most important role may be to balance out the power among the conflicting parties so that negotiation can proceed based on the fundamental issues involved (Halverstadt 1991, 78).

The conflict manager's attention should be focused on facilitating quality communication, restoring the balance of power, and facilitating the use of power in a way that will enable the church to fulfill the Lord's mission.

FROM THE PASTOR'S DESK . . . *One the most graphic metaphors or images of the Church in the New Testament is the apostle Paul's description of the Church as the Body of Christ. In the midst of Paul's teaching about spiritual gifts, he writes to the Corinthians: "For even as the body is one and yet has many members, and all the members of the body, though they are many, are one body, so also is Christ" (1 Cor. 12:12, NASB). The apostle continues to describe how important all of the members or body parts are to the physical body, the foot, the hand, the eye, and the ear. And he says, "The eye cannot say to the hand, 'I have no need of you'" (v. 21, NASB); and he concludes that every member of Christ's Body has value, gifts, and a God-given purpose.*

This is a compelling picture of the interconnection and interdependence of the members of the Church. The scripture makes clear what the world would miss with its love of power and celebrities. Even the weakest link in Christ's Body has something of value to contribute and communicate. Leaders who are pressured to find generous financial gifts to underwrite the budget and to recruit the best talent in town to grace the platform and classrooms must never forget that humility and servanthood are still the foundation for authentic Kingdom work. And our communications system is to include all who are impacted by the conflict that comes to every church.

When I met with a church board following the call to be the pastor, I asked what the mission statement was, and not one leader could give one line or even the concept from the purpose statement. They said they knew the church had one on file and suggested I ask the associate pastor or business manager for a copy of it. I knew that my first year as pastor would involve working with those leaders to write a mission statement they would own and hold one another accountable to fulfill.

Our Lord knew we would get a lot more accomplished for the Kingdom together than we could apart. And we can stay together if we love one another sufficiently to analyze the sys-

tems and the relationships that will enable us to avoid conflict over the minor matters and give ourselves to passionate prayer and open discussion of whatever will empower us to major on our main mission.

8

FAIR FIGHTING; DIRTY FIGHTING

Once conflict actually breaks out in a church, interested parties will become strident in their efforts to pursue their own goals and will begin to employ various fighting strategies to try to make sure their side wins. The use of fighting strategies is neither unethical nor unchristian, it is a normal part of human behavior as people attempt to resolve differences among themselves.

Contrary to what Christians are often taught, there are actually some positive aspects to "fighting" in relationships. It can often "clear the air and bring suppressed problems into sharp focus" (Ury 1999, 177).

While we take the position that fighting can be healthy, the tactics used can be either ethical—which we will call *fair fighting*—or unethical—which we will call *dirty fighting.*

Getting the church to use fair fighting strategies is important for building Christian community in the way it resolves differences. A strong Christian community is built through a process that develops year to year, not something that is accomplished overnight. Fair fighting strategies utilized today will create the environment for healthy approaches to conflict in the future.

FAIR FIGHTING

Church conflicts are best resolved when the interests of all parties are given full and equal consideration. When individuals feel that their interests have not been represented in reaching a final decision, they are not very likely to be supportive of those decisions. They may be secretly resentful that they were not respectfully heard out, and this may sow the seeds of discontent and future conflict. Those who choose to fight fair not only want their own interests represented but also want the interests of those who disagree to be expressed as fully and clearly as their own, believing that this is the way the community will arrive at a quality decision that all members can support.

Halverstadt takes the position that assertiveness—not aggressiveness—is the key to fair fighting in church conflicts (1991, 91). It is important that people be given the tools and encouragement to develop the skills necessary to speak up for themselves and their ideas in church meetings so that those who are decision makers can hear the interests of everyone who will be affected by their decisions.

Those who are committed to fair fighting want to be certain that all ideas are expressed openly and fully so that outcomes are not determined by intimidation or misrepresentation or other dirty fighting tactics. They believe that all interests should receive equal treatment rather than some interests receiving preferential treatment over others.

Fair Fighting Tactics

People who fight fairly are open about expressing their own thoughts, feelings, and interests. They accept themselves as people of worth, created in the image of God, who have a valuable and important role to play in the church. They fully accept Martin Luther's concept of the priesthood of the believer, embracing that every ministry role in the church is important and everyone's input is worthy of consideration if the church is to arrive at solutions that will help it achieve its mission.

Fair fighting means taking ownership for one's own ideas and feelings. Individuals should be willing to take ownership of their own ideas by stating, "I think . . ." or "I feel . . ." rather than "Some people think . . ." or "I know others feel . . ." when that person is really expressing his or her own thoughts or feelings. Bystanders or the conflict manager should strive to empower all parties to represent their own interests, but those who fight fair will do their best to avoid speaking for others.

Fair fighting means holding oneself accountable to others in the church for one's own words and actions. Everyone makes mistakes, and everyone is sometimes inconsiderate of others. Part of the discipline of the Body of Christ is to help us know when we have committed an offense so that we can make amends. Those who fight fairly are concerned about justice in

A person interested in fair fighting listens carefully to what the other person has to say.

the Christian community, believing that justice is most fully carried out when we make ourselves accountable to the common good. A person interested in fair fighting listens carefully to what the other person has to say, possibly seeking the counsel of others in determining whether some injustice has been done.

Fair fighting means addressing interests, positions, and behaviors rather than personalities. Disagreements that focus on personalities deteriorate into competitions that result in some people winning and others losing. When the community deals with conflict by addressing underlying issues, this will work toward arriving at a solution that will meet the needs of broader church constituencies, taking the focus off personalities.

DIRTY FIGHTING

It would be ideal if all parties involved in church conflicts would pursue a win-win approach that protects the interests of all involved. It is safe to say that this is not the approach most often utilized. Unfortunately, there are many parties to church fights who choose to use *dirty fighting* tactics, adapting a win-lose attitude.

"I do not understand what I do. For what I want to do I do not do, but what I hate I do" (Rom. 7:15). Paul's statement characterizes well those who use dirty fighting strategies in church conflicts. They know what they are doing is wrong, but in their minds the conflict has reached a level that they must use whatever means available to win—even if those means are unethical. The risk of losing the fight somehow seems greater than the risks of violating ethical standards.

In understanding why people choose dirty fighting tactics, it is important to examine the context in which the church conflict occurs. When individuals in the church are losing their jobs in the secular world, when churches are in danger of closing, or when church leadership positions are being eliminated and finances are a serious concern, the likelihood increases that dirty fighting tactics will be used (Halverstadt 1991, 83). These sorts of threats make people more defensive, and unethical methods of winning are easier to justify.

The tendency to employ dirty fighting tactics to drive out fair fighting is a problem in church conflicts. Sometimes it's necessary for the conflict manager to intervene to prevent this from happening.

To simply say that the ends do not justify the means will not dissuade dirty fighters. They are convinced that the goals for which they strive are honorable, perhaps even essential to the church achieving its mission, and according to their distorted thinking, any means they choose will serve the best interest of the church.

Dirty fighters sometimes justify their tactics by rationalizing that the other side has more power or the command of more resources. At other times it is those who have the most power who choose to fight dirty because they believe that damage will be done to the church if the other side wins the battle, and they think almost anything is justified.

Dirty fighting takes the focus off of the basic issues and puts it on factors such as personality, power, and influence. Important resources that should be directed toward the business the Lord has given the church to do are now directed toward achieving selfish and personal ends that are often in contradiction to what the church should be doing.

Dirty Fighting Tactics

Refusal to be open with others is a dirty fighting tactic, particularly when information is kept from others in the conflict that could have a significant impact on the choices or decisions made. For fair fighting to take place, all parties must work to openly address the issues before the church without pursuing hidden agendas that are designed to deny the open participation by all church members whose interests are at stake.

"**Character assassination** is the usual mode of attack in church fights" (Leas 2001a, 27). While those who use this tactic may not be willing to admit it, the basic purpose of this tactic is to hurt, demean, or even destroy the other party to the conflict. The use of character assassination moves the conflict to a very harmful level for both the parties involved and the church itself.

Relationships within the church are damaged for a long time after a bitter conflict in which character assassination has been a major fighting strategy. People are not willing to make themselves vulnerable to others when their character has been maligned in a past conflict. Relationships are strained, resources are heavily guarded, and the church cannot carry out its ministry.

Repressive tactics to prevent others from having their interests shared with those involved in the conflict is another dirty fighting strategy. This silencing strategy is sometimes used to:

- Limit the alternatives considered so one's own appears to be the most desirable.
- Keep the decision makers from discovering weaknesses in one's own position.
- Keep others from gaining recognition that could lead to them developing a basis for leadership.
- Suppress comments that could be construed as critical of one's leadership or contribution to the church.

These repressive tactics may actually have the appearance of legitimacy when carried out through maneuvers in parliamentary procedure that keep those representing opposing positions from participating in the discussions. Repressive tactics can also be veiled threats or actual punishing behaviors directed at those who have taken opposing positions. Perhaps those who disagree are threatened with loss of leadership positions or pastors are reminded of impending church votes on pastoral renewal as strategies for getting one's own way through repressive means.

Divisive language is a means of carrying out several other dirty fighting strategies in church conflicts (Halverstadt 1991, 105-6). A common one is the use of *we/they terminology* in an effort to make it appear that the opposition is a group of outsiders who do not really belong in the church. Language is purposefully used to divide, to put up barriers, or to make others feel as though they are not really in tune with the majority of church members.

Another dirty trick is *name calling*, which is a form of divisive language in which a label is attached to the opposition that the dirty fighter knows is grossly unfair. Labels may be words like "hypocrite," "unchristian," or other words that demonize people in the eyes of others in the church, taking the focus off the issues and placing it on prejudice against certain individuals that have been labeled.

The use of *deception or deliberate lies* is another harmful trick that occurs when one party to the conflict untruthfully reports what the opposition thinks, has said, or is planning to do. The lies are used to get people upset with the opposition and create the impression there is really more danger to the church than is actually the case.

Those who use unethical means of fighting also may resort to *intimidation tactics* with those with whom they are in conflict. They interrupt others who are speaking, invade their space by standing too close to them, use a loud voice or other communicative behavior intended to dominate anyone who differs with them.

Refusal to be accountable to others for the manner in which one engages in conflict is another dirty fighting tactic. These individuals may set themselves up as a "law unto themselves," sometimes taking extreme actions such as "taking the church's financial records, changing the locks on the doors, barring entrance to meetings, starting competing congregations, disrupting meetings, and suing the congregation in civil court" (Leas 2001c, 18).

It will generally take intervention from bystanders to restrain those who employ dirty fighting tactics. It requires individuals representing the church as a whole to confront them about their behavior and insist that these behaviors stop.

FROM THE PASTOR'S DESK . . . *Charles Swindoll, in his* book The Grace Awakening, *tells about the Quaker who owned an ornery cow. Every time he milked her, it was a clash of two wills. One particular morning the cow was unusually irritable, but the Quaker was determined to endure the session without any harsh words. As the farmer began to milk her, Ol' Bossy stepped on his foot with all of her weight. He struggled silently, groaned a little under his breath, pulled his foot free, and then sat back down on the stool. She then switched her tail in his face like a whip. He merely leaned away so it would not be able to reach him. Next she kicked over the bucket, by then half full of warm milk. He started over, mumbling a few words to himself; but he never lost his cool. Once finished with the ordeal, he breathed a sigh of relief, picked up the bucket and the stool, and as he was leaving, she hauled off and kicked him against the barn wall 12 to 15 feet away. That did it. He stood to his feet, marched in front of his cow, stared into those big eyes, and he shook a long, bony finger in her face and shouted, "Thou dost know that I am a Quaker. Thou dost also know that I cannot strike thee back. But I can sell thee to a Presbyterian!" My apologies to all Presbyterians. Don't threaten people with whom you have differences. The Lord allowed Barnabas and Paul to have differences, and He will allow you and your church to have disagreements without resorting to worldly or carnal weapons.*

To avoid the conflict that would harm the church, it is important that the pastor or conflict manager teach the group or perhaps the entire congregation that certain behavior is inappropriate in the midst of church disagreements. It is always wrong to misrepresent the truth or to exaggerate or lie and then justify such behavior because there is some important principle at stake.

Some destructive tactics can be avoided if leaders will consistently follow the constitution or bylaws of their governance or the local church's policies that have been established over time to avoid behavior or decisions that would harm the church *body. As a denominational executive of a large group of churches, I once met with a church board that had already assumed responsibilities that the bylaws of the denomination assign to the denominational executive. When this section of the constitution was brought to their attention, they replied that they did not follow the church polity. If I as a leader had been inconsistent and followed the bylaws when it benefited me and disregarded them when it was not to my advantage, then I would have been on shaky ground. But since I gave my best effort to consistently follow those guidelines, I was on good ground to fight fairly with these local leaders. The result was that the previous actions were rescinded, and the church board operated in accordance with denominational governance.*

Neh. 5 teaches about conflict management. Nehemiah knew the conflict during the building of the wall at Jerusalem after the Exile could blow up in his face, and the wall would never be built. God's chosen people were fighting against each other and manipulating one another. There was definitely some dirty fighting going on in and around the Holy City.

Leaders must know that this kind of internal conflict is worse than an outside enemy. When church members fight each other unfairly, it tears them apart and distracts them from the main mission, which for Nehemiah and God's people was the building of the wall to protect the city of Jerusalem.

Nehemiah, in a time of crisis, became the conflict manager who had to confront those who were fighting dirty. And in all organizations there are times when a leader has to step out and confront behavior and attitudes that will be damaging to the cause of the Kingdom. Nothing will undermine the mission of the church quite like a church fight that gets out of hand and leaves casualties and hurts that will be a stumbling block to the church at present and for generations to follow. May God give us both wisdom and courage as leaders to know when to confront or restrain dirty fighting while enabling the conflict that will help the church grow and fulfill the biblical mandate.

9

COMMUNICATION SKILLS FOR CONFLICT MANAGERS

THE MOUNTAINVIEW CHURCH

The Mountainview Church's history was marked with triumphs as well as tragedies. When George Martin accepted the call as pastor of Mountainview, the church was rebounding from its most recent tragedy.

Ten years earlier the congregation was blindsided and devastated when their popular pastor was suddenly removed for "conduct unworthy of a minister of the gospel." His credentials were removed, and he left the ministry but continued to live in the community. A few congregants and a couple of board members were still in frequent contact with him. The next pastor was there for only a short time, feeling unaccepted by the membership.

The next pastor, the one who immediately preceded George, was there for eight years. During his ministry the attendance had climbed back into the upper 400s. The board made it clear to him that it wanted the church to grow to 800 or 900 in attendance. While there were those who were obviously pleased with the growth, the pastor heard continual comments that compared him unfavorably with the pastor who had been removed. There were suggestions made to him that he later learned had been relayed to him from that pastor. It was obvious that the removed pastor's influence was still strong in the church. Even though he led the church through a building program that provided a much-needed education and fellowship wing, the criticism and comparisons continued, and he left for a larger church in another part of the country.

After becoming the pastor, George Martin wondered if he would have accepted the call if he had known the whole story. He felt strongly, though, that the Lord had called him to Mountainview, and he had a vision for growing this church to become a major force for the Lord in the community.

During the first year at Mountainview, George kept all three existing pastoral staff members. One of them had served the church for over 15 years. But George saw many signs that another staff member, the minister of music, had never really disconnected from the pastor who had been removed. The minister of music seldom acted on suggestions George made for changes in the music ministry, and changes he did make were later found to have been at the suggestion of the former pastor.

When George released the minister of music, two board members and a significant number of others were very unhappy. They continued to be quite vocal about their displeasure.

Church attendance slipped somewhat after the music minister was released, but the number who left is considerably smaller than the number of new people in the church.

George considers team building one of his strengths. In each of the churches he has pastored, he successfully built a strong sense of teamwork in the pastoral staff. That sense of teamwork is developing now in his second year at Mountainview, and George is gratified by the united front the staff now presents to the church. He loves the members of his staff and feels a deep commitment from each of them. The staff member who has been there for more than 15 years is a particularly strong advocate for George.

George's vision for Mountainview is "Teams Working Together for Christ." His messages challenge people to ask themselves, "What team am I on?" and "What is my team doing to reach this community for Christ?" When he meets with members of various groups, such as the teenagers, he asks them the name of their team and asks them what their team is doing to reach other teens.

George has dealt with significant problems, however. A recent problem surfaced when his wife let him know that one of the board members, Martha, was complaining to members that the church services didn't seem to be as evan-

George told Martha that he had been with the church almost two years now and was interested in how she thought things were going.

gelistic as they had been under previous pastors. George immediately called Martha and asked if they could meet at his house after the evening service on the following Sunday. Martha agreed.

When Martha arrived on Sunday night, George's wife served cookies and coffee and then discreetly left the room so that George and Martha could talk. George told Martha that he had been with the church almost two years now and was interested in how she thought things were going. He told her that his reason for requesting her to come to the house was because he wanted to know if there was anything in particular that she felt should be discussed.

"Well, now that you mention it, there is something. You know that I've been a part of this church for most of my adult life. I remember over the years the many times I've seen people going to the altar at the close of our service. I remember the night I stepped out at the close of a service, and my life has never been the same. To be frank, Pastor, since you've been our pastor, we just don't seem to have those evangelistic services much any more. I really miss that."

"I appreciate your honesty, Martha," George responded. "I know you don't have a critical spirit, and I can see that this is something important to you. If you don't mind, I'd like to share with you how I see the Lord using me at Mountainview."

George went on to share his vision of how the Lord is using his gifts in team building to reach the community. He reminded Martha of the training sessions on friendship evangelism where members learned how to share their faith with their friends, and he gave her several examples of new people in their church who were there because a member had shared his or her faith with them.

Martha thought quietly for a moment, then said, "Pastor, you're right about new people coming into the church. But couldn't we have both friendship evangelism and evangelistic services? Why does it have to be one or the other? If we had both, maybe even more people would come."

"My theory is that we all should be involved in the evangelistic program of the church," George replied. "I don't want all the evangelism left up to me. That's why I put most of my efforts into preparing the members to reach out to their friends and neighbors. I think right now I have the ministry balance that best suits the spiritual gifts the Lord has given me. I'd appreciate it if you would put together a team to join me in praying for the Lord's leadership with regard to our church services. I can think of a couple of people who would be interested in being members of that team if it sounds like a good idea to you."

Martha agreed to head up the team, and the pastor asked her to have the team pray about what role the church services should serve in reaching the community for Christ.

PREPARING TO COMMUNICATE

A great deal of the effectiveness of communication is determined ahead of time. Communication skills are significantly enhanced by careful preparation.

1. Is the person with whom you intend to communicate a "parent"? If so, who are the "children"? Or is he or she a "child"? If so, who is the "parent"? Is he or she an "independent child"? (See chapter 6.) In our example, the fact that Martha is a board member does not necessarily mean she is a parent in the church's family structure. But if she is a parent, it is likely that the people to whom she has been complaining are her children in the church family structure, and George will want them to know that he and Martha have met and agreed on a strategy for addressing their differences.

2. What is the person's role in the church's communication system? As a member of the church board, Martha holds a central role in the system. How this conflict is handled could have significant positive or negative implications for the church.

3. At what level is this conflict? (See chapter 4.) Are there widespread conflicts among church members regarding the church services? Pastors and other leaders are continually amazed at how quickly conflicts spread. George believes this particular conflict is at a low level. When conflicts have escalated to levels four or five, involving the other party in a task force to work on the problem is seldom effective.

4. What are the deep interests of those who are in conflict? In his conversation with Martha, George became convinced that this conflict was a legitimate concern of Martha's and was not driven by the agenda of the former pastor. His strategy for communicating with her is shaped largely by this knowledge. If the agenda was driven from outside the church, another strategy would have been necessary.

5. What is the relationship of the conflict to the vision you believe the Lord has given you for the church? The goal is for conflict to become a means of transforming the church so that the vision becomes reality. George keeps his focus on that vision as he works through the conflict. If Martha's concerns resulted in the board telling George he needs to put more effort into evangelistic services, his vision could be jeopardized.

COMMUNICATION SKILLS

Conflict is threatening to people. They feel threatened with the loss of the familiar, with the possibility of personal attacks, or with harm coming to people they love. They feel threatened with rejection by others in their church.

When people feel threatened, they become defensive and try to protect themselves. One of the

When people feel threatened, they become defensive and try to protect themselves.

ways they protect themselves is by closing down to people they think might hurt them. The only people they are open to are people they feel they can trust. The people they most need to be in contact with are those with whom they have significant differences, yet these are precisely the people they try to avoid.

When people aren't communicating with the ones with whom they have conflict, the information received is usually either second-hand or thirdhand and full of rumor and distortions about the issues and the people involved. This results in bad decisions built on misinformation, making the conflict worse and more destructive. It becomes a downward spiral that deteriorates. This is why it is so important for those in conflict to have good communication skills.

Active Listening

The most critical communication skill when dealing with conflict is active listening. Active listeners pay careful attention to both the words and the nonverbal behaviors. Pastor George, in the situation presented here, was impressed with the sincerity of Martha's concern about the services. He may have picked up both verbal and nonverbal communication signals on which to base his impression.

On the *verbal* level, Bob noticed that Martha described her own personal experience. She described deep, personal feelings about an evangelistic service that was a turning point in her life. She didn't describe how other people feel about the situation such as, "A lot of people are unhappy about the changes you have made in our church services." She didn't use a Billy Graham crusade as an example, which would be very different from the situation in their local church. She didn't use win-lose language—"Either the services change or I am leaving and taking a lot of people with me"—to describe her feelings. Her words didn't indicate a need to win a battle with the pastor. Rather, she showed genuine desire to do what will bring people to the Lord.

Nonverbal signals need to be interpreted in terms of the person as a whole and not as isolated incidents.

George probably also noticed the *nonverbal* ways in which Martha communicated. He knows it is easy to badly misinterpret nonverbal signals, so he was careful about the meaning he attached to them. Nonverbal signals need to be interpreted in terms of the person as a whole and not as isolated incidents.

The pastor detected a warmth in Martha's voice and, although she didn't make much eye contact with him, he interpreted that as her way of protecting herself from seeing his disappointment when he heard what she had to say. He observed the same warmth in the expression on her face. If her facial expression had been hostile or tense, George would have been on the defensive and would not have made himself vulnerable to Martha.

George demonstrated active listening by reflecting back to Martha what he heard her saying. This convinced Martha that he was really listening to her and not just giving her an opportunity to express herself in the hope that would be enough to keep her happy.

Reflecting is an especially important communication skill when dealing with conflict. It is important to say to the one with whom you are discussing the issue, "Now, let me tell you what I hear you saying, and you tell me if I have it straight."

George's active listening was demonstrated most of all by his recommendation that Martha form a team to pray about the direction of the services. This says to Martha that he is open to serious consideration of doing things another way.

Unfortunately, those with whom a pastor is in conflict will not always address the situation in warm and open ways. If someone is yelling at you, the inclination will be to yell back. But if you can control your emotions and communicate concern and understanding to the person who is on the attack, the emotional content of the situation can be lowered substantially.

Assertiveness

Assertiveness is not the same as aggression. Assertive people seek to advance their agendas while showing regard for the agendas of others as well. Aggressive people push their own agendas

Sometimes parties in conflict don't want intervention, but the conflict has potential to do such harm to the church that the leader must intervene.

without regard for the welfare of others.

Pastors surveyed emphasized the importance of addressing conflict as early as possible. This requires assertiveness on the part of the pastor or lay leaders. It's tempting to ignore conflict in hopes the parties involved will somehow resolve it and the conflict will go away. If, however, intervention is needed and doesn't happen, the conflict will be much harder to deal with when the leader is finally drawn in.

Sometimes parties in conflict don't want intervention, but the conflict has potential to do such harm to the church that the leader must intervene. The assertive leader will intervene in a way that communicates to all that the primary concern is the church's mission. The leader must demonstrate that when the church's mission is advanced, the interests of all are valued.

Assertiveness is also needed when people who wield power in the church are taking advantage of those who have no power. Sometimes lay leaders need to be assertive with pastors who use their power to overwhelm those who differ with them. Confronting others in love as set out in Eph. 4:15 is an important skill for the leader attempting to manage church conflict. If a party to the conflict is employing dirty fighting techniques, it may fall to the conflict manager to confront that person to discuss the harmful effects his or her tactics are having on the church and other members. The conflict manager should be careful to describe the person's behaviors and its effects rather than accusing or blaming the person. He or she also will want to communicate a deep respect and concern for the person, knowing that the dirty fighting tactics may grow out of scars or wounds that have been carried for many years.

Reframing is a strategy the conflict manager can use to change members' perceptions of the nature of a conflict. For instance, if reductions are needed in programs or personnel, the conflict manager can help members put a "pruning" frame on the discussions as opposed to one that highlights decline or deterioration. The effective conflict manager uses his or her communication skills to put a positive frame on conflict. This increases the possibility of a positive outcome.

Timeliness, clarity, and accuracy will be hallmarks of the successful conflict manager's efforts to keep all parties informed as he or she guides the church through the conflict management process. It is important that all involved receive accurate information when they need to know it in a clear, well-organized format.

Hundreds of years ago, a Roman rhetorician said the crucial question is not whether your message can be understood but whether it can be misunderstood. This is still an excellent question for conflict managers to ask themselves today. "Is it possible for my message to be misunderstood and, if so, in what way can I express it that would reduce misunderstandings as much as possible?"

Redundancy improves the likelihood that accurate information will get through to church members. If there is an important meeting coming up to discuss some aspect of the conflict, it should be announced at least twice both orally and in writing. This strategy also provides evidence that the conflict manager is working hard to keep all church members informed during the process.

Don't tell people not to be angry or upset (Leas 2001a, 44). The conflict manager wants to know how people are feeling as well as what they are thinking. If you tell members not to be angry, you are signaling that you are not concerned about the anger they feel or the reasons for that anger. Suppressing anger will not resolve the conflict. Resolution will come when that anger is dealt with in a positive manner.

Don't accuse people of negative motives (Whetten and Cameron 1998, 338). As an example, let's say one of the parties to a church conflict stands up during a meeting and charges that the pastor is not accountable enough to the church for his or her actions. If the conflict manager responds in a way that appears to accuse the member of "grandstanding" for personal benefit rather than for the purpose of resolving the conflict, it could be a very serious mistake.

The conflict manager is making an assumption about why the person spoke up in the meeting—an assumption that may or may not be true. It is not possible to observe motive; therefore, any statement made about someone's motives are inferences that could be untrue and unfair. Also, while the person's statement may have caused discomfort for the pastor and others, the person may have been speaking for a sizeable contingency in the church and felt this was the appropriate time to make the statement. Finally, making such a statement before the whole congregation could serve as a catalyst for getting all parties to recognize that there is a problem that needs to be addressed.

The effectiveness of the conflict manager's communication is the key to establishing and maintaining relationships with all parties to the conflict. The quality of these relationships will determine the quality of the information and support he or she receives from the parties to the conflict.

FROM THE PASTOR'S DESK . . . *I once attended a class on conflict management, and as a case study was presented to the class, one of the pastors in attendance tearfully confessed that he identified so strongly with the example that he didn't feel he could respond without personal bias. Just the night before he had attended a church meeting where hurtful things were said about his leadership, his ministry, and even his family. We wondered how he could have attended the class with the weight of all the baggage he brought with him. Suddenly we realized that this was a God moment, and we gathered around our fellow pastor and laid hands on him and prayed for healing, peace, and for God-anointed answers for the conflict he faced in his church.*

The pastor of the church cited in this example in chapter 9 is to be commended for his boldness in casting his vision for the future for team building to reach the community for Christ. He was also wise in communicating with Martha, listening to her concerns, and then enlisting her to lead a team to pray and work to enhance the evangelistic vitality of their worship services. I have discovered in my own pastoral ministry that when I prepare carefully crafted questions and think through the positive affirmations I can communicate with authenticity, the much better the outcome.

The anointing of God's Spirit is available for communicating vision from the pulpit as well as empowering the one-on-one encounters with key leaders who have a contribution to make in moving vision to reality.

10

MEDIATION

Jane is a relatively new member at Elm Street Church. Shortly after completing the membership class, she was elected to the church board. She is a young professional who is very popular with other young people in the church.

Jane's profession is financial planning, so she was obviously interested in the financial statements that were distributed at the first board meeting she attended as a new member. Almost immediately Jane realized that the financial statements were difficult to read and didn't follow standard accounting principles for presenting information on a balance sheet.

Right after that first board meeting Jane approached the senior pastor, David, to share her concerns about the treasurer's report. She asked David if he felt the church treasurer, Alex, would be open to her offer to help in organizing the financial statements. David told her he had been concerned about the financial statements since becoming pastor five years ago, and when he asked Alex questions in that regard, Alex was not very forthcoming in answering his questions.

David went on to tell Jane that Alex might not appreciate the implication he needed help with the financial records, and if she decided to offer her assistance, she needed to be careful not to give the impression that she didn't think he knew what he was doing. David also shared with Jane that the church was about to submit a loan application for financing for the new church annex. He was concerned that the financial records might not be in order, jeopardizing the chances of getting the loan.

David reminded Jane that Alex's brother, Scott, is also on the church board and suggested that Scott might be willing to ask Alex if he would like Jane's help with the extra work of getting the financial documents prepared for the loan application. Jane liked that idea and told David that she would contact Scott about doing that.

The very next Sunday morning, three board members approached David and asked if he knew that Jane had raised questions about Alex's abilities as church treasurer. They saw no reason Jane should question Alex's competency to do a job he had been doing for 10 years and wanted David to speak to Jane and ask her to leave Alex alone. David agreed to speak with her.

When David reached Jane, she was clearly upset. She told David that when she talked to Scott and asked him to talk to Alex about her offer to help prepare the financial documents for the loan application, he told her that he would talk to Alex, but that Alex was very well organized and probably wouldn't need her help.

About the time the three board members were talking to David on Sunday morning, Alex, Scott, and another board member confronted Jane and told her they resented her raising questions about the job Alex was doing as church treasurer.

Alex accused Jane of wanting the job of church treasurer and talking behind his back to the pastor and other board members. She tried to assure Alex that she didn't want his job and was only trying to be helpful. She told him that the pastor had suggested he might want some help preparing the loan application. Alex then asked her pointedly if the pastor had expressed doubts about the way the treasurer's job was being handled. At that point, Jane realized the conversation was getting out of hand and told Alex that she would find some other way to be helpful to the church family and that she didn't really think they should discuss it any further.

"Did the pastor tell you I have been treasurer for 10 years and that the church is in good financial condition?" Alex asked.

"Alex, I said I don't want to talk about this any more," Jane replied, and she turned and walked away.

After reporting this conversation to David, Jane told David that she felt hurt and angry that she had been attacked in this way when she was just trying to help the church. David told her he was sorry she had to go through that and promised to talk with Alex.

Within hours David was confronted by a group of young professional people in the church who expressed their displeasure about the way Jane was being treated by the church board. They wanted Alex to apologize to Jane and give Jane access to the financial records to see if they were in order. They reminded David that as members of the church they were entitled to see all financial records as well as to appear at a board meeting and call for an outside audit of the records. They told David that was exactly what they intended to do unless Alex invited Jane to look over the records. David realized it was time for him to invite Alex for a talk.

THE PASTOR'S POSITION IN THE CONFLICT

David can see two coalitions building, with Alex as the "parent" of one "family" and Jane as the parent of the other. Alex's coalition is made up of longtime members who also happen to hold the majority of positions on the church board. Alex has used his position as treasurer to build a strong power base. The "children" in his family are in influential positions that he has helped them get and keep. Alex is always a member of the nominating committee and frequently chairs that committee.

The second family is made up of young professionals who are relatively new members. They hold Jane in high regard and look to her for leadership. It was their votes that were chiefly responsible for her election to the church board. They consider the other coalition—or family—as control freaks who don't want younger people in leadership positions. They are angry that these older members seem to be more interested in hanging on to their power than in seeing the church grow. And they are very angry about the way Jane is being treated by this more powerful coalition.

The church communication system has a high concentration of power in Alex's family. Therefore, the two coalitions are out of balance—a situation that is not conducive to successful negotiation. David must find a way to put the two coalitions in balance to reduce the tendency for either side to begin using dirty fighting tactics. When the powers are in balance, the parties are much more likely to fight fairly.

> *When the powers are in balance, the parties are much more likely to fight fairly.*

Although David doubts the young professionals would carry out their threat to appear at a church board meeting to demand an independent audit, they should not be taken lightly because the threat is an early warning signal that they intend to be heard. The advance warning may be a sign that they have confidence in him and the church's decision-making process to protect their interests. If they conclude their confidence is misplaced, dirty fighting tactics may appear.

The fact that a contingent of church board members approached David at the same time another contingent confronted Jane should signal him that Alex's coalition has launched an offensive to protect their interests. They may only desist when the opponent has been defeated or driven out, which bodes ill for the church.

One result could be that Alex's "family" will become a clique that runs the church with occasional "guerilla attacks" from those who are not part of the dominant group. If the clique has sufficient power—which it appears to have at this time—those who are unhappy will eventually leave the church. The church will become a revolving door of people coming in, getting frustrated, and leaving. The church's growth and mission will be seriously jeopardized.

Another result could be that the group of young professionals will become strong enough to mount a serious challenge to Alex's coalition. Such a challenge could consume the whole church, forcing everyone to take a side, eventually splitting the church.

Whether David realizes it or not, he does not have the luxury of confronting this conflict while it is still at a low level of intensity. It likely is already a level three conflict, meaning he should seriously consider seeking outside help. Elm Street Church is independent, so there are no denominational authorities to go to for assistance. It would be advisable for David to consult other veteran pastors or contact a church conflict consultant for advice.

David is not a party to the conflict yet. His job right now is mediating between Alex and Jane. He needs to create an environment where both of them feel safe in negotiating the conflict for themselves. This won't happen overnight. In the meantime, all parties must accept a level of uncertainty while the conditions are created in which Alex and Jane can negotiate with each other in love.

David realizes that the church board may soon be aligned against him if it becomes known that he is unhappy with the way Alex is handling the church treasurer's job. He feels that he has been drawn into a no-win situation between the two coalitions. At this point he cannot choose whether or not he will be involved in the conflict; he can only choose his role in it, and even that may not be totally within his control.

If David is successful in his mediation between the two coalitions, a conversation between Jane and Alex in which they negotiate directly will eventually take place. But first, David's efforts will be directed toward coaching them in the use of fair fighting tactics. If he can get them to commit to that, then they can begin to negotiate directly. Ideally, the process will begin by repairing their relationship so that they can focus on the issue of church finances without attempting to overpower or outmaneuver each other.

MEDIATION PRINCIPLES

1. The Christian conflict manager can intervene with a rational, creative problem-solving process under the guidance of the Holy Spirit to move the conflict toward resolution (Halverstadt, 8). David cannot wait for the conflict to play itself out. This unmanaged conflict could eventually destroy the church and perhaps even end his career.

2. David's task is to develop a positive relationship with Jane and Alex as individuals so that he can coach them into repairing their relationship. To get drawn into their relationship is to risk triangulation where both Jane and Alex attempt to use David against each other.

3. There may be "independent children" in the church who could be helpful to David in achieving a successful resolution to the conflict. These members will be independent thinkers with skills and resources they can use to protect the church. David must focus on the system as a whole rather than allow his attention to be narrowly directed to the fight between the two coalitions.

> *After the parties have built a relationship of trust and respect with each other, they can focus their attention on the issue.*

4. After the parties have built a relationship of trust and respect with each other, they can focus their attention on the issue. It would be counterproductive to address the issues before that relationship is established. If the conflict manager concludes that the parties are not able to successfully repair their relationship, it may be necessary, as a last resort, to move from mediation to arbitration in which an outside agency imposes a solution on the church.

5. Church members tend to lose sight of the important reasons the church came into being in the first place when the church is experiencing internal conflict (Leas 2001a, 12). The church's mission should be stressed to all parties involved. Members are not asked to forget about their own interests, but they are asked to pursue their interests in a way that benefits everyone.

6. Getting to the resolution of a conflict is a gradual process in which sometimes what appears impossible at the beginning seems almost natural at the end (Ury, 181).

7. Conflict managers should focus more on the parties' interests than on their positions (41). David should be more concerned about Alex's and Jane's needs than on their opinions regarding church finances. If he shows them he can and will protect their interests, they will feel safe in negotiating their positions.

David decided that it was time for him to speak with Alex and asked him to come to the church office. He began the conversation by telling Alex he was very concerned about the conflict that was occurring between him and Jane. When Alex voiced his belief that Jane was trying to take his position of treasurer, David tried to assure him that no one wanted that to happen. He went on to express his concern that there would be major repercussions for the church if this matter wasn't settled. He told Alex that he was going to set up a committee of members who were not involved in the conflict to help bring good from it.

"Why do you want to bring other people into it?" Alex asked.

"Because," David explained, "this is a matter that affects the whole church. I don't believe other members would want to sit by and watch this fight tear our church apart."

"Then why aren't you working through the church board?"

David explained, "Because it's obvious that most of the board is already involved in this conflict. I need members who are not committed to either side. We need to set up a process to protect our church and bring some good out of this."

Alex angrily informed David that the board members were going to be very unhappy. He accused David of never wanting him to serve as church treasurer. He informed David that the church board was going to have a thing or two to say to David about the way he was handling his job as pastor. With that, he got up and walked out the door.

David is really in need of help at this point. Alex was clearly threatened by the process of bringing other members into the situation, and he continued to use accusation and blame to deal with the conflict. The danger level for David and the church was rising.

David called a veteran pastor that he respected to discuss the situation. This pastor agreed that David was doing the right thing by bringing other respected church members in to help.

Marshaling the Forces on the Sidelines

The battling coalitions in the Elm Street Church represented a significant portion of the church's leadership and membership, but not all of it. David approached two members he knew to be wise, spiritually grounded individuals who contributed significantly to the church.

Joyce worked part-time as administrator at a senior citizen center in town and taught a Sunday School class for older adults. She was not part of any particular clique or coalition in the church. David considered her to be a thoughtful, compassionate person who cares about the community and people.

Matt was a high school biology teacher who had devoted a lot of his time to the teen group in the church. His spiritual development over the past several years as well as the leadership he had shown with the teens was well respected. He had been a board member in previous years but decided to have his name left off the ballot in the last board election. Matt had been helpful in dealing with a previous conflict between a group of teens and some board members over how the teens were using church facilities.

David met privately with Joyce and Matt to share his concerns about the emerging conflict. He began by asking them to keep their discussions in the strictest confidence. Once they agreed to his request, David told them about the struggle developing between longtime church members and the newer, younger members who wanted to offer leadership but had been rebuffed. He told them about the threats and dirty fighting tactics being used by both sides. David told Joyce and Matt that their job was not to decide the conflict but rather to set up and monitor a process that would ensure that all parties fight fairly so that the conflict could be brought to a successful resolution.

Joyce and Matt agreed to help David and also recommended that he recruit two or three other church members to join them, which he did. David ended with a conflict resolution task force of four to work toward bringing good out of the conflict. He set up a board meeting on the following Sunday to introduce the task force and invite the members to suggest procedures the task force could use.

The Board Meeting

The next Sunday David introduced the conflict resolution team to the church board. Following are his comments to the board:

"I'm very concerned about a conflict that is developing in our church that has the potential of doing great damage to our church and its mission. A church fight could derail the progress we've been making and cause some people to leave the church. I don't think anyone in this room wants to see that happen. Jane isn't here, and I'm sure that isn't a coincidence; I didn't see her in church this morning, either.

"I've been approached by two different groups about this developing problem. One group—which consists of many of you—is upset because you respect the job Alex has done as church treasurer and you think Jane is questioning his work. The other group is upset because they think some of you ganged up on Jane and accused her of doing things she didn't do. Both sides are accusing and blaming, which is not the way to handle this situation.

"I have asked Matt, Joyce, Tim, and Jerry to serve on a conflict resolution task force to help me protect our church as well as bring good out of this. I believe conflict can be good for our church, but it has to be handled very carefully. If we all go into this just trying to defeat the other side, our church is in trouble. If we go into it with the idea of making something good happen for all of us, we will be better off after the fight than we were before. It all depends on whether or not we are willing to put the mission of our church ahead of our own personal interests. These four people are going to try to help us make something good happen."

One of the board members asked why Jane and Alex couldn't just work it out without getting anyone else involved. David explained that he hoped someday the two of them would be able to sit down and discuss the financial records of the church but that right now that probably couldn't happen. He explained that they had to work on straightening out their relationship before they could talk about finances.

One of the board members wanted to know if Jane and Alex and the pastor could sit down and get this straightened out. Another board member asked Alex if he would feel more comfortable if someone besides the pastor sat in on his and Jane's discussions. Alex said that he would, so David asked the conflict resolution team to work with Alex and Jane to find someone outside the church to help them by acting as facilitator when they met together.

The pastor ended the meeting by asking the board to leave the problem in the hands of the conflict resolution team, Jane, and Alex so that the process could work.

Analysis

Let's look at some pointers we can take from the Elm Street Church conflict.

- The pastor took the warning signs seriously and selected a mediation process appropriate for the level of danger he believed existed.
- David accepted responsibility for his part in creating the conflict by not addressing his concerns about the financial records years earlier. He further complicated things by telling Jane that he had questions about Alex's performance.
- Bringing other members into the situation helped bring the power between the two coalitions more into balance.
- Bringing in an outside mediator between the two parties increases the probability of success—although it doesn't guarantee it.
- David, knowing that Alex doesn't trust him, was agreeable to bringing in an outside party to facilitate the conversation between Alex and Jane. This may be painful for David, but he was committed to doing what was best for the church.

This conflict was not resolved at this point. Alex may still have another power play up his sleeve. Jane hasn't agreed to the process and may already have made up her mind to leave the church. The important point is that a process based on fair fighting has been set in motion. It is equally important that the process has been endorsed by the church board and others in positions of influence, and this well help ease uncertainty and tension in the church.

Now the church must wait and rely on the willingness of the parties to cooperate, the skill of the outside facilitator, and the help of the Lord to bring power out of pain.

FROM THE PASTOR'S DESK . . . *Leaders may decide to delay a response when they become aware of interpersonal conflict between church members, but when finances are involved, the very integrity of the church may be called into question. This conflict cannot be ignored.*

Pastor David is to be complimented for his prompt action and good decisions once the conflict became evident. He was assertive and thorough in pulling together key components that will hopefully lead to eventual resolution of the conflict and save the church from serious fracture.

The process supported by the church board and the conflict resolution team will hopefully keep the church safe from destructive conflict, and the Elm Street Church will emerge even stronger as it pursues the mission the Lord has given its members.

11

NEGOTIATION

The conflict at Elm Street Church is potentially damaging to the church, the members, and Pastor David. In the hope that good for the church could come forth from the conflict, a conflict consultant, Martin Brown, was called in.

David held a meeting in his office with Marty and gave Marty as much information as he knew about the conflict and its origins. He acknowledged mistakes he made that very well may have caused the conflict to grow, and he filled Marty in on the roles of the key players. He told him about the meeting with the church board, establishing the task force, and the fact that Alex had agreed to meet with Jane if someone was brought in from the outside to mediate. He also mentioned that Jane was not in church Sunday and had not attended the board meeting, so she was unaware of the task force and that Alex had agreed to meet with her. It was a clear concern to Marty that Jane had not attended church or the board meeting, and he said he would make an effort to talk with Jane as soon as possible.

David and Marty then had a long discussion to give Marty the background of the church's history, some general information about the church's political structure, and other information to help Marty understand the conflict. Marty asked a lot of questions about both Alex and Jane. He wanted to know about any previous conflicts in which they had been involved as well as how well they tended to get along with others in the church.

Marty then talked about what he saw as David's role in the conflict. He told him that as much as possible it would be good for him to stay out of the conflict. Marty indicated, however, that there might come a time when David would have to take a stand on how the church finances are handled. He told David that he would let him know if he saw such a time approaching so that David could prepare to address the issue. Marty commended David for bringing the other church members into the situation when it appeared the conflict was escalating and for seeking the advice of a veteran pastor on the approach he was taking.

Marty also told David that it had probably been a mistake to send Jane to Scott rather than going directly to Alex. Another alternative would have been for David to approach Alex directly himself. Either way, it would have been best to address the matter without getting other board members involved. One of these options likely would have allowed David to clear things up with Alex without setting off the power struggle between factions in the church.

At David's request, the church secretary set up a meeting between Marty and Jane at a local coffee shop for later that day. Marty introduced himself and told Jane that he had been contacted to help the folks at Elm Street Church work through this conflict. Their conversation went like this.

"Is this really so serious that someone from the outside has to help us?" Jane asked.

"Well," Marty answered, "there are some serious charges and threats being made, and when a conflict gets to this level, the church usually needs some help. The pastor isn't taking this lightly. Did you know that Alex agreed to meet with you to try to work this out?"

"Yes, I heard," Jane replied. "As soon as he apologizes for ambushing me with his friends, I'll consider meeting with him. Until then, there isn't much for us to talk about."

"I take from your comment that you would be open to repairing the relationship with Alex, then. Is that right?"

"Are you saying I'd have to be the one to repair the relationship?"

"No, not at all," Marty answered. "It would be something the two of you would do together. I'd be there to help you, but it would be up to you and Alex to do the work."

"The way things are in that church, I'm not even sure it's worth the effort," Jane replied.

Marty asked her why she felt that way.

"The way I see it, even the pastor is powerless to do anything about it."

"That is Alex's own little kingdom over there. He controls the nominating committee and the finances. No one is going to get any significant position in that church unless they're willing to do just what Alex wants. The way I see it, even the pastor is powerless to do anything about it."

Jane acknowledged that she still felt a lot of anger and hurt over being confronted by Alex and his friends. Marty agreed that the three of them converging on her after church was wrong. He told Jane he felt the first order of business was to repair the relationship with Alex. If that was successful, then they could work on other issues she wanted to raise.

Jane agreed to think and pray about it.

After meeting with Jane, Marty set up a meeting with the conflict resolution task force. He wanted to keep them informed of every step taken in working through the conflict. Marty asked David to be present in the meeting also.

When Marty met with the task force he asked them to sign a form agreeing that they would not share with anyone else the things that were discussed among them. He then explained the following principles that he employs in helping churches deal with conflict.

1. He is not there to resolve the conflict for them. He is there to help the people directly involved resolve it for themselves.
2. He is working for a *triple win*—a win for each party involved and a win for the church. He doesn't want anyone to come out a loser.
3. His specific measures of success are:

- Reduced tension
- Improvement of problem-solving strategies
- No loss of members and/or return of lost members within 18 months
- Decisions made will be honored for two years (Leas 2001b, 5)

Marty informed the task force that Jane and Alex were not ready to meet together at this point—especially as far as Jane was concerned. He explained that it might be necessary for him to meet with Jane several times before she would be willing to meet with Alex. He said that he wouldn't set up a meeting between the two of them until he felt certain it would produce a positive outcome.

One of the task force members asked Marty why Jane was unwilling to meet with Alex, and Marty explained that Jane was very hurt and angry and felt she had been ambushed by Alex and two other board members. She felt that all she was doing was trying to help and that she had been accused of trying to steal the treasurer position away from Alex.

Marty went on to tell the task force that it was important that they understand that there were issues beyond the way the church finances were being reported. He explained that the young professionals that were new members of the church felt they were being blocked from leadership positions, and if this issue wasn't resolved, the church would become a revolving door with new members coming in the front door and going out the back. He told them that the basic question to be answered was whether or not Elm Street Church was ready to change.

"Who's blocking them from leadership?" one of the task force members asked.

"Jane sees that she is the only young person on the board. She also sees Alex as always on the nominating committee and usually chairing it. In her opinion he is controlling the finances, and she feels he is also controlling who gets into church leadership positions."

"Maybe we should have board members rotate off the board every three years or so," suggested Tim.

"That's really not up to us to decide," Jerry replied.

"That's right," said Marty. "But a conflict resolution task force has several

A conflict resolution task force has several responsibilities.

responsibilities. One of them is to make recommendations on how the church can avoid conflicts like this in the future. You may want to recommend to the church board that a review of the church's organizational structure is warranted."

"Pigs will fly before that happens," Jerry retorted.

"I hope that's not the case," Marty said. "Because if it is, the board better be prepared for a group of Jane's friends to show up at a board meeting and demand an external audit of the church's books."

"Do you think they would really do that?" Matt asked.

"When people think their legitimate concerns are not being addressed through normal channels, they will resort to raw power moves," Marty explained.

"Aren't the church's books open for any member to look at?" asked Joyce. "Jane can see the books anytime she wants, can't she? After all, she's a member of the board."

"Well, actually," David looked down in embarrassment, "Alex keeps them at home."

"I didn't know that," Jerry objected. "Those books should be kept in the church office. Pastor, I think you need to tell Alex to bring them back to the church."

"I'm meeting with Alex later today," Marty said. "I'll talk with him about it."

When Marty and Alex got together for their meeting, Marty introduced himself and thanked Alex for meeting with him. Alex shared with Marty his feelings regarding the conflict and acknowledged to Alex that he didn't want to see anything bad happen to his church. Marty asked him what bad things he wanted to avoid. Alex said he didn't like people fighting, particularly in church, and that the reason he had agreed to meet with Marty and Jane was in the hope of stopping the fighting.

"If Jane was sitting here with us tonight, Alex, what would you say to her?" Marty asked.

"I'd ask her why she's trying to take the church treasurer job away from me and why she's talking behind my back. By the way, why isn't she here meeting with us?"

Marty told Alex that Jane was hurt and angry and that she still wasn't ready to meet with him. He talked about his role as conflict consultant and explained to Alex that he would also be meeting with Jane to discuss her thoughts and feelings on the conflict. He acknowledged the church's strong financial position and complimented Alex on the job he had done as church treasurer. Alex told Marty that he had never had formal accounting training but had drawn on his experience from running his own business.

"You are to be commended for the fine job you've done, Alex," Marty said. "Do you mind if I take a look at the books?"

It would be easy for all involved to just throw up their hands and go to another church.

"I don't keep them here," Alex admitted. "I keep them at home. If anyone has a question about the finances, all they have to do is ask and I'll get an answer by the next board meeting."

"Alex," Marty asked pointedly, "why don't you keep the books in the church office? Don't you think that's really where they belong? The board members seem to feel strongly that the books should be available to them."

Alex reacted angrily and suggested that the board was trying to take his job too.

"Alex, no one is trying to take your job. Everyone is trying to do what is best for you, Jane, and the church. It would be easy for all involved to just throw up their hands and go to another church. But if that happens, everyone loses. Sacrifice and forgiveness are the only things that will get us through this. Tell me honestly why you don't keep the books at the church."

"I know where every penny of the church's money is," Alex answered. "I never took an accounting course, and I probably don't show it the way the accountants would want me to, but I'm proud of the job I've done for my church."

"Alex, you have every right to be proud. The pastor and the church appreciate the good job you've done and the hard work you've put into it. But Jane wants to do her part too. She can help by showing you how to put together some of those reports. Really, Alex, that's all she wants to do."

"To tell you the truth," Alex answered, softening, "I was getting nervous about the loan application. I was afraid the bank would ask me questions I couldn't answer. Deep down, I know I need some help. I'll have the books in the church office tomorrow morning."

For now, Marty's strategy is to uphold the ideals of love, sacrifice, and forgiveness and let Alex and Jane apply them to their own lives. The conflict manager will allow the parties involved the opportunity to do the loving, sacrificing, and forgiving for themselves. Only if they show an unwillingness or inability to do this will the manager become more direct in calling for such action. Accusing or blaming is seldom the way to get people to change their behavior. The manager must model the approach he or she wants the parties to take.

Marty has prepared the way for repairing relationships, but some fundamental issues remain, such as the concerns that Jane and her friends have about access to leadership positions. Before Marty can move on to any other issues, though, he must persuade Jane to meet with Alex. He has prepared Alex to come to the meeting with an apology, but now he must get Jane in the frame of mind to accept the apology.

Jane agreed to meet with Marty again in the same coffee shop. After exchanging greetings, Marty asked Jane what she had been thinking and feeling about the conflict in the last several days.

"Oh, I don't know, Marty. I guess I'm just not sure it's worth all the stress I'm feeling right now. I feel like church should be a place where I can get away from some of the stress of my job, not just add to it."

Marty agreed with Jane about that but added that he'd had a very good meeting with Alex and felt that Alex was ready to do his part to repair his relationship with Jane. When Jane asked if Alex was going to apologize, Marty said that he would not ask Jane to meet with Alex if he thought Alex was going to verbally attack her again but that he preferred to let Alex speak for himself.

Jane agreed to meet with Alex and asked if Marty would be there. He assured her that he would.

> *This is our chance to demonstrate that love, sacrifice, and forgiveness are what we're all about.*

"Let me ask you this," Marty continued. "If you and Alex meet and you're able to make a new start on a good relationship with each other, are there other issues you want to discuss with him?"

"That's for sure," Jane replied. "I think it's important that the church not go back to business as usual. I think the newer, younger people in the church should at least have the opportunity to be considered for leadership positions. Otherwise, they're going to move to other churches. The thing is, I wonder if that might be what Alex wants—to make it impossible for new members to feel involved so that he can just keep things the way they've always been with him running just about everything."

"I don't think Alex would be willing to do his part in repairing the relationship if that was the case," Marty said. "We have to be a little patient with him. He's feeling unappreciated right now. This is hard for him, just as it's hard for you. As I told him, this is our chance to demonstrate that love, sacrifice, and forgiveness are what we're all about. If we can demonstrate those three things, I think we can work this out so that everyone feels good about it."

The next evening Marty, Jane, and Alex met. Both Jane and Alex were a bit nervous and ill at ease when they entered the room. Marty attempted to make them feel a little bit more comfortable and then tackled the issue that had brought them together.

"I want to thank both of you for coming here. By agreeing to meet together it shows that both of you want to do what's right for your church and for yourselves.

"Basically we're here for the two of you to talk to each other. I plan to stay mostly in the background. If I feel I need to step in at some point, I'll do that. If that doesn't seem to be necessary, then I'll be quiet. If either of you thinks you need my help, feel free to ask me for it.

"There are just a few ground rules that I'd like for you to abide by. First, please speak only for yourselves. Avoid saying things like, 'Many people in the church think . . .' or 'Some people say . . .' That won't help get to the root of the problem and solve it. Each of you needs to own up to your own thoughts and feelings and speak only for yourself.

"A second guideline is to describe how you're thinking and feeling rather than making accusing statements to the other person. It's important that you try to see this conflict from the other person's perspective. If you stick to talking about how you see the situation, that gives the other person the opportunity to understand what you have at stake.

"Do these guidelines seem reasonable to both of you?"

Jane and Alex both agreed that they did.

"Do either of you have other guidelines you'd like to suggest?" Marty asked. Neither of them did.

"OK, then, let's begin. Alex, based on the talk you and I had earlier, would you like to begin?"

Alex at first stumbles over his words and looks down at the table. As he begins to talk, though, he becomes more comfortable. Jane also is looking down at the table, but shortly after Alex starts talking, she looks directly at him. It is obvious from the beginning that Alex is conciliatory.

"I apologize for the way I've treated you," Alex begins. "It was wrong of me to say the things I said to you that Sunday after church. I'm sorry." Alex now looks up at Jane.

"Thank you, Alex," Jane responded. "I'm partly to blame for not going up to you right after the board meeting. I didn't know you, and I didn't know how you'd respond. I really am not after the treasurer's job, Alex. It's obvious to me that you've taken good care of the church's finances."

"That really means something coming from you, Jane. Thank you. If you could find the time to meet with me, I'd really appreciate it if I could ask you some questions about keeping the books and putting together the treasurer's report."

"I'm sure I could. I'd like to help in whatever way I can," Jane said. Jane's tone belies the fact that she's not feeling quite as relieved as Alex feels, but Alex begins to make motions like he thinks the meeting has come to an end. Jane doesn't say anything, so Marty intervenes.

"Before we go, Alex, I think there's something else Jane would like to talk about. Is that right, Jane?"

"Yes," Jane replied. "Alex, I'm sure you've noticed that there are quite a few younger people like me who have started coming to Elm Street Church. We all appreciate what you and other longtime members have done to build up the church. But it appears to me that there just isn't much opportunity for newcomers to get positions of leadership in the church. What would you think about having church board members rotate off after serving three or four years so that newer church members could have more opportunity to serve?"

Alex's tone now changes markedly. "Jane, don't get me wrong. I'm really glad we have new people coming to the church, and we need new members. But I think it's the people who have been around for a long time who should be in leadership positions. We're the ones who really know the church and have worked hard to make it what it is.

"When Scott decided not to run again, that opened up the opportunity for you to get elected. But I don't think it's right to take a job away from somebody just because they've been in that job for three or four years. What if we ended up with all new people on the board? I think things are fine just the way they are."

"But, Alex," Jane objected, "to the new people it looks like you control the finances as well as who the church leaders are because you're always either on the nominating committee or you're the chairman of it."

"Marty," Alex turns to Marty, "I don't want to start another fight. I'm afraid if I say anything else it'll come out wrong or I'll be misunderstood. I think I've made my position pretty clear. I hope Jane and I can work together on getting the church's books in shape, but on these other things, we'll just have to agree to disagree."

Marty concluded the meeting with a prayer and thanked Jane and Alex for their willingness to meet. He told them he would report the outcome of the meeting to the Conflict Resolution Task Force and to the pastor.

When Marty met with the pastor and the task force, he reported the following:

- Jane and Alex repaired their relationship.
- Alex will return the church's books to the church office.
- Alex and Jane will work together to get the financial records in shape and to prepare the loan application.

Pastor David and the task force were very pleased with what had been accomplished.

Marty was disappointed to have to tell them that Alex wasn't open to relinquishing control of the finances or the nominating committee.

"Alex feels that the people who have put long years of service into the church know it best and should be rewarded for the years they've put into building the church into what it is today," Marty reported. "He thinks new people should be considered for positions as they come open but that no one should have to give up a job after a certain number of years.

"At any rate," Marty continued, "I don't think you folks need my services any longer. The conflict intensity level has decreased substantially, and I don't think anyone is going to storm a board meeting. Now you'll have to deal with how you'll govern your church. I think the folks in this room are very capable of determining how to proceed from here."

After Marty left the meeting, Pastor David told the task force that he was sure their work was not finished. He said he was convinced that the organizational structure of the church must be opened up or it would lose most of the new people. He asked the task force to work with him to put together a new structure. He said he would tell the church board what he was planning and ask board members for suggestions as to what the new structure should be.

Two of the board members were very unhappy when the pastor shared his plans with the board. One of them accused him of trying to bypass the people who were duly elected to make decisions for the church. David told them that the ultimate authority was with the membership as a whole and that a matter of this magnitude should be taken directly to them. One of the two disgruntled board members attempted to start a behind-the-scenes move to have the pastor removed but gathered little support, and he has since left the church.

> *There were no threats or confrontations, and people spoke their minds in the church meetings with all members given a fair hearing regardless of how long they had been members.*

Two years have now passed, and the church has been working with a new organizational structure for a year. In the new structure, the church board members rotate off the board after serving three years and may then be elected to serve again after one year. The nominating committee consists of the chairs of the major church committees, which are elected positions. Since the new bylaws do not allow the church treasurer to serve as the chair of the finance committee, Alex is no longer on the nominating committee.

David was pleased with the way the church made the transition to the new structure. There were no threats or confrontations, and people spoke their minds in the church meetings with all members given a fair hearing regardless of how long they had been members. The new structure passed the congregational vote by a fair margin. As far as the pastor knows, the disgruntled board member is the only person who left the church because of the change.

Jane and Alex have a good working relationship. Jane has taught Alex many accounting practices that he can use in handling the church books. And Jane has learned a lot from Alex about the early days of the church and the sacrifices that were made to keep the church going when things were difficult financially.

The Elm Street Church is a transformed church. The relationships between members, the way the church makes decisions, and the quality of those decisions are all improved because those involved in conflict chose to love, sacrifice, and forgive.

ANALYSIS

Marty, the conflict consultant, realized that his services were needed only as long as the conflict was at a level the church could not control. Once the conflict level was reduced, it is much better if those directly involved in the conflict take responsibility for bringing the situation to a resolution. If the church consistently turns to outside help to solve every conflict, the church will not grow and develop in its ability to manage conflicts, develop strong relationships, and make quality decisions.

Pastor David exerted real leadership in handling this potentially explosive situation. He recognized when it was time to call in outside help, and he realized that his own involvement in the conflict made it impossible for him to successfully mediate between Jane and Alex. He also decided at two critical points to bypass the church board and go directly to the church membership as a means of balancing out the difference in power between the new people and those already in power.

David chose to work within the church's legitimate decision making. He formed the task force that resulted in a recommendation to the congregation for action, and he was willing to accept the consequences of the church's decision.

Marty intervened in the negotiation between Jane and Alex only when it appeared that they were not going to get to one of the basic issues about which Jane was concerned. It is not uncommon for those without power to feel too intimidated to bring up the points they want to see addressed. Sometimes they just leave the church to avoid confrontation. The mediator's role is often to support those who are overpowered and restrain those who are overpowering.

This case demonstrates how difficult it is to transform a conflict into positive energy that will move a church toward achieving its mission. In this instance the pastor recognized his limits and also recognized when leadership was called for. The mediator was able to handle a high level of emotional intensity with calmness and confidence. But most importantly it was the willingness of those involved to be forgiving and to ask forgiveness that moved this conflict to a resolution that was good for the church.

FROM THE PASTOR'S DESK . . . *Marty Brown had just the right balance of toughness and tenderness to intervene in a difficult chapter of the history of Elm Street Church. He spoke the truth in love and brought caring, warmth, and understanding to the conflict. As an outside consultant he moved in like an evangelist and with the Spirit's help created an environment where forgiveness and reconciliation could repair a broken relationship. Marty then wisely stepped back and let the pastor deal with the next issue of opening up the leadership to newer members.*

This model is the ideal every leader hopes and prays for when there is major conflict afoot that can do great damage to the church.

Many years ago I faced a similar scenario, but the strong, powerful leader decided to leave the church. A few close friends of his joined him, and a new congregation was planted in a growing community 10 miles away. Today it is a vibrant, growing church.

The departure of some of the leaders opened up leadership positions to a group of young adults who then led an evangelistic thrust into the community resulting in the building of new facilities to accommodate the growth. Looking back, I see now how God used what appeared to be failure to resolve the conflict to transform the pain into bold plans for building the Kingdom.

Paul and Barnabas, in the New Testament, had disagreements and even went their separate ways. But the conflict didn't keep them from risking their lives to achieve the mission that eventually turned the Roman world upside down. May we all be so devoted to our Lord that we are ready to be the servant leaders who will display love, sacrifice, and forgiveness to further the kingdom of our Lord Jesus Christ.

12

CONFLICT RESOLVED

Tim Johnson was the pastor of the Broad Street Church for 10 years. During his tenure the church's membership grew from 50 to 150 with Sunday morning worship attendance averaging about 225, making the sanctuary comfortably full. Most of the growth, however, occurred during the first 7 years of Tim's ministry with little or no growth occurring over the last 3 years. While this was of some concern to Pastor Johnson, he reasoned that the fact there was little room for more people in the sanctuary may have caused the church's growth to reach a plateau. Tim suggested to the board that it might be time to start holding a second Sunday morning service, but there appeared to be little interest in doing that among the board members.

Tim was also aware that some folks in the church were unhappy with a recent decision he made concerning the Barnabas adult Sunday School class. Sharon Allison was the teacher, and the class had grown to about 40 people in regular attendance on Sunday mornings. Pastor Johnson talked with Sharon about the possibility of dividing the class so more people could participate in discussing the lesson. He also noted that attendance had leveled off, and his study of church growth suggested that dividing the class could be a stimulus to a resurgence of growth. The pastor asked Sharon to discuss the matter with the class members and let him know their feelings.

Sharon reported back a couple of weeks later to tell Pastor

Johnson that there was a significant difference of opinion among the class members as to whether or not the class should be divided. Sharon didn't have a strong opinion one way or the other, saying that she could see reasons both for and against dividing the class. She suggested that the pastor take the matter to the Sunday School board for its input.

Pastor Johnson did discuss the matter with the Sunday School board, but there was no consensus on the issue. Tim felt a decision needed to be made, so he decided that the Sunday School class would be divided.

Pastor Johnson was aware of another possible problem lurking just below the surface that concerned his personal lifestyle. Tim and his wife, Laura, always dressed very well, as did their children. He bought a new car every three years, usually an expensive model that was out of reach for most members of the congregation he served. Although he had never been confronted on this issue, every once in a while Laura told him that she had perceived some discontent regarding the lifestyle they enjoyed.

Tim had one friend in particular, Mike Bryant, whose counsel and friendship he counted on. Mike was a former evangelist selling insurance for a large company in the area. He taught a Sunday School class and served on the church board. Tim felt Mike was someone he could talk to about matters pertaining to church. Mike was very careful never to speak with anyone else about the things he discussed with the pastor.

At coffee one morning, Tim decided to talk to Mike about his concerns that some members were not happy with him as their pastor. Tim was reluctant to bring up the subject, but he respected Mike's opinion and really wanted to know what Mike thought about it.

After Tim shared his concerns with Mike, he asked Mike if he also felt there were people in the membership who were displeased with his performance as pastor.

"Well," Mike replied, "if you're saying there are some people who don't agree with your decisions, I think that's always going to be the case. You'll never be able to please everyone."

"That's not exactly what I mean," the pastor responded. "I get the impression that some folks think I should let the board make more decisions rather than

Part of my problem is that I don't even really know which people are unhappy.

making so many decisions myself. But when I make decisions, I'm always careful to talk with people like you and Sharon Allison before I decide. Sometimes I also ask the board as a whole for its opinion before I decide. I just see my position as pastor as one of a leader who sets the direction for the church."

"Tim, I really couldn't say how many people are unhappy about that. I know some are, but that's to be expected. I think you just have to do what you feel is right and lead according to what you think is best for the church. Your approach to leadership is certainly biblical from my point of view. That's not to say it is the only biblical approach, but it certainly is one of them."

"Part of my problem," Tim continued, "is that I don't even really know which people are unhappy. If I knew who they were, I'd go talk with them."

"If you don't know who they are," Mike said, "you can't really be sure anyone's unhappy. I heard there were some people who were really unhappy about your decision to divide the Barnabas Sunday School class. But I also realize that the class was getting too large, and you explained your reasons for doing it. It's just that some people really didn't like that."

"But I asked Sharon to discuss it with the Sunday School class, and there was no consensus on what we should do. Even Sharon said I should go ahead and do what was best for the church. When I asked the Sunday School Board, it was divided on what should be done. I just made my decision based on what I thought was best for the class and for the church."

"And you did the right thing," Mike responded. "As I said earlier, you're not going to please everyone all the time."

"Do you think I should meet with the folks who are unhappy about the Barnabas decision?" Tim asked.

"I don't know," Mike said. "You're not going to put the class back together based on what they have to say, are you?"

"No."

"Then it's probably best to just let it go and not get their hopes up."

About two weeks later, Sharon Allison came up to Pastor Johnson before the start of Sunday School classes. She told him that she and a few other people would like to meet with him after the morning service. Tim asked what topic was going to be discussed, and Sharon said they wanted to talk with him about the future of the church.

Tim was understandably anxious about what would transpire at the meeting, and he immediately sought out his wife and told her of his discussion with Sharon. Laura hadn't heard anything about it and didn't know any more than Tim did. Tim thought about finding Mike Bryant before the start of Sunday School, but then he remembered that Mike was out of town and a substitute teacher was going to be teaching his class. He went to his office, shut the door, and prayed that the Lord would help him preach that morning and calm his anxieties about the meeting planned for right after the service.

Tim preached quite a good sermon in spite of his concern. He thanked the Lord for His help and was grateful that concentrating on the sermon helped him keep his mind off the meeting.

Immediately following the service, Tim greeted people at the door. He was concentrating so completely on talking with the people as they left the sanctuary that he paid no attention to the number of people gathering at the front. When he turned to head back to his office, he was stunned to see a group of about 30 or 35 people gathered in the front pews. He went immediately to meet with them. They were all sitting in the first three rows, and he stood before them.

"I understand you folks want to meet with me," Tim said.

Sharon Allison was obviously the spokesperson. She remained seated as she spoke. "Pastor, there are some other members of our group who wanted to be here this morning but couldn't. There are probably 10 or 15 more who had to miss because of other commitments.

"After a lot of prayer and discussion, we've decided that we'll be starting another church. We want you to know that this isn't a decision we've reached lightly. For some of us, this has been our church home for more than 10 years. We know we'll be leaving behind people who have become some of our closest friends. But we're convinced this is the right thing for us to do. We know you didn't know this was coming, so we don't really expect you to say anything right now. We just didn't feel right about writing this to you in a letter or leaving without saying anything. We knew we had to share this with you face-to-face. It's our prayer that the Lord will continue to be with this church and bless it, and we pray He'll bless our new church. This will be our last Sunday here."

The pastor was in such shock, all he could say was, "Thank you for sharing this with me in the way you have." He then turned and walked back to his office. He closed the door and wept.

After about half an hour alone in his office, he went home and shared what had happened with his wife. She was equally upset, and they wept together. Tim and Laura didn't realize that this wasn't the last shock they would face. One more loomed ahead of them.

As the day wore on, many questions began to come to mind. Who was behind this? Who would pastor the new church? What would the denominational leader for the district think and say about all this? Did he even know? Was it done with his approval? Why did these people want to leave the church? Was this all because of splitting the Sunday School class? Surely not. Where would the new church meet? Would even more church members leave when they found out what was happening? Was this the end of Tim's ministry?

Tim decided to call Mike Bryant first thing on Monday morning to get together and talk about what was happening. He knew Mike could help work through his feelings and would have suggestions for somehow getting these people to reconsider their decision. Maybe Mike would agree to meet with the group and begin a process of getting the church back together.

Tim wasn't able to catch Mike before he left for the office the next morning, but he had Mike's cell phone number. He'd never called the number before because he didn't want to disturb Mike while he was working, but he decided this was a unique situation.

When Mike answered, he was driving to a meeting with an out-of-town client about an insurance matter. He immediately recognized the pastor's voice.

"Good morning, Tim. I thought it might be you calling."

"I guess you heard about what happened at church yesterday," Tim said.

"Yes, I did."

"Is there a chance we could get together sometime today to talk about it?" Tim asked.

"I won't get back into town from meeting with this client until late tonight. But there's something I need to tell you. First, I want you to know that I had nothing to do with organizing this group or the decision to leave the church."

This was the first time Tim had heard the phrase "leave the church." For some reason, those words had a much harsher ring than "start a new church."

"So what you're saying is," Tim asked, "this is not so much a move to start a new church as it is to leave my church."

Mike was obviously jarred by the question; the uncertainty in his voice spoke volumes to Tim.

"Tim, please don't take this the wrong way."

"How am I supposed to take it when 50 people stand up and say they're leaving my church? Is this supposed to be something I'm excited about?" For the first time, the pastor began to feel angry over what was happening.

"Tim, what I need to tell you is that last Sunday night the group came to me and asked me to be the pastor of the new church. I prayed about it all week, and Saturday night I told them I would be their pastor."

The anger was intensified by feelings of betrayal and disbelief. Tim had no idea what to say; he simply hung up the phone.

When he gained his composure, he went home to talk with

Laura. Again, they wept together. "How could he do this to me?" Tim asked, not really expecting an answer. "He was my friend. I told him everything. I trusted him."

Tim decided it was time to call the district superintendent, Rev. Kenneth Jackson. After getting Rev. Jackson on the line, Tim told him about the shock he had received the day before after the morning service and about the second shock he had received that morning. "Do you know anything about this?" Tim asked.

"I have no idea what you're talking about. Tell me what's going on."

Tim recounted the events as they had transpired.

"Rev. Jackson, some of these people who are leaving are major leaders and financial supporters. How could they be so unhappy without me knowing anything about it? I just can't see how I can go on pastoring this church. Who knows how many other people feel the way they do? How can I go back there and preach to that congregation next week when everyone knows a major portion of our church has left?"

Rev. Jackson listened carefully. "Tim, first I want to say that I'm so sorry you have to go through this. I can only imagine what you're feeling right now, and I know it must be terrible. Let me pray with you." Rev. Jackson then prayed for the Lord's presence and healing in the lives of Tim and Laura and their children. He could hear the weeping in Tim's voice on the other end of the line.

"Thank you, Rev. Jackson. I just can't believe that Mike Bryant agreed to pastor that church. He and I met regularly, and I shared so much with him about my concerns. I guess that wasn't such a good idea."

"I wouldn't say that," Kenneth answered. "We need to get together to talk. I'm going to clear my calendar for tomorrow, and I'll drive down to spend some time with you and Laura. Will you be available if I get there about ten o'clock in the morning?"

"Yes, we will," Tim responded. "I can't tell you how much I appreciate you driving down here to see us."

Tim and Laura spent the remainder of the day talking, crying, and praying. Tim wished he could talk with someone in the church who could help him understand what was happening. Laura told him that she had no idea there was such unrest in the congregation. She was feeling more and more angry about the way her husband was being treated.

Toward the end of the day, Tim called the church secretary and asked her to call a special meeting of the church board for Wednesday evening. He felt that regardless of the outcome of the meeting with the district superintendent, he wanted to talk with the remaining church board members about what had happened. Maybe they could help him understand why this had taken place.

Rev. Jackson spent four hours with Tim and Laura. He told Tim that he would contact some of the people who left the church to help him determine what had happened. He did not hold out the possibility to Tim and Laura that they might come back. He knew that when people take drastic action like this, they seldom come back.

As Rev. Jackson prepared to leave, he asked to pray with Tim and Laura. Tim spoke up. "Rev. Jackson, before you pray, there is something I need to say. Laura and I have talked and prayed about this a lot, as you can imagine. I have to tell you that my confidence in my own ability to pastor this church is deeply shaken. I thought things were going well. Attendance had leveled off, but I thought that was because of our facilities. I guess I should have known something was wrong when the board wouldn't even discuss the possibility of a second worship service. But I never saw anything like this coming.

"I've asked the church secretary to call a meeting of what's left of the church board for tomorrow night. I plan to tell them that I don't believe I can lead them out of this crisis. I just can't lead people when I don't know what they're thinking and feeling about me. I have no idea what we're going to do, but I'm not interested in being assigned to another church. I think it's best that I take a break from the pastorate and figure out whether this is really what God wants me to do. I'm not at all sure it is."

"Don't you think you should take some more time to think and pray about this?" Rev. Jackson asked. "I'm afraid you're making this decision based mostly on how you feel right now. I don't want you to rush into a decision you'll regret later."

"You may be right, but I know I can't continue to lead this church. I'll tell the church board that this is the way I'm leaning. Then I'll take another week to think and pray about it and let you know what we've decided. This is as much Laura's decision as it is mine."

"What will you do? How will you support your family?" Rev. Jackson asked.

"I have no idea. But I believe the Lord will provide for us."

The next evening Pastor Johnson met with the remaining church board members. "I know you all probably know by now why I called this meeting. After church Sunday morning a group of about 35 people from our congregation asked to meet with me. They said there were about 10 or 15 others who could not be at the meeting. I have since received a list of 52 people who are part of their group. They told me that they've decided to start a new church. In other words, they're leaving our church. They asked Mike Bryant to be the pastor of their new church, and he has agreed to do that. I have to tell you that I'm deeply shaken by this. I just can't believe that all this was going on behind my back, and no one came to me to tell me about it.

"Yesterday, Laura and I met with the district superintendent. I told him that I don't believe I can continue to lead this church under these circumstances. He asked that I not make a decision based on my emotions, so I agreed to take a week to continue to think and pray about it. Laura and I won't be here on Sunday, so the pulpit committee needs to find someone to preach. I'll let you know what we decide, but I think you should know that you may need to begin the search for a new pastor."

A week later Pastor Tim Johnson submitted his official letter of resignation as pastor of the Broad Street Church. Tim's brother managed a large department store in a nearby town, and he offered Tim a position as the appliance department manager, and Tim accepted. Tim and his family moved out of the large, spacious parsonage into a small apartment. After working for his brother for two years, he accepted a position as the manager of an auto parts store in the same town for a significant salary increase.

As Rev. Jackson began to understand the situation more clearly, he saw that there was no way those who left the church would return. He initiated the process of searching for a new pastor for Broad Street Church. Tom Anderson was called as the new pastor, and the church began to grow.

At the same time, the new church pastored by Mike Bryant began to grow. Mike continued to pastor the church for about three years, and then he went back into the insurance business. The new pastor got along very well, and even though they remained smaller than the Broad Street Church, new people continued to come at a steady pace. Six years after the group splintered from Broad Street Church, the total attendance of both churches was significantly larger than that of Broad Street at the time of the split. Both churches flourished spiritually and continued to grow.

One day Tom Anderson made a phone call to Tim Johnson.

"Tim, this is Tom Anderson, pastor of the Broad Street Church."

"Hello, Tom. I understand things are going very well at Broad Street. You must be doing something right over there."

"Well, I thank the Lord for His goodness to us. I was wondering if you and I could get together for lunch someday soon."

"If you're hoping I can help you with a problem at the church, Tom, I don't think I'm the one you should be asking."

"Oh, no. I would just like to meet you for lunch."

Tim agreed, although in his heart he felt some reluctance. What Tim didn't know was that Tom was feeling a call to move on to another church. During the time he had been at Broad Street, he realized there was a core group of people there who really loved Tim as their pastor. Tom's goal was to get Tim to come back to Broad Street Church as its pastor.

A couple of weeks later, Tim and Tom got together at a restaurant near Tim's work.

"Tim, I've been the pastor at Broad Street for about six years now, which I'm sure you know. I'm really feeling like I have accomplished what the Lord had for me to do there. I'm telling you this in total confidence, Tim, because other than my wife, I haven't told this to anyone. I don't see myself at Broad Street Church for more than another year or two.

"I don't know whether you knew it or not, Tim, but no one else left the church six years ago other than those who met with you that Sunday morning. Those who remained were terribly sorry to see you leave as their pastor. I know that must've been an awful experience for you, and everyone understands that you did what you felt you had to do. But I'll tell you right up front that my goal is to see you come back as the pastor at Broad Street."

"It's great of you to come here and tell me this," Tim responded. "But that's really out of the question. I'll never put me or my family through anything like that again. With the Lord's help and a wonderful wife and family, I've worked through that situation. It's behind me."

Tom continued to meet with Tim. After a period of about two years, Tim began to feel that the Lord was calling him back to Broad Street. At first Laura was very hesitant. "The Lord may be calling you," she told Tim, "but He sure hasn't told me!"

Tim began to pray earnestly for a clear sign from the Lord as to what he should do. His work at the auto parts store was going well, and the owners were pleased with his work. He and Laura had bought a home, the nicest home they'd ever owned. Deep inside, though, Tim knew that he was not fulfilled in this line of work.

One day Tim received a call from Rev. Jackson, the district superintendent. Rev. Jackson asked to meet with Tim and Laura. When he was face-to-face with them, he told them that Tom had announced his resignation to the members of the Broad Street Church. He also told them that he had met with the church board about securing a new pastor. He said that he had come to tell them that the church board had voted to put Tim's name before the congregation for a vote. The church board's unanimous recommendation to the congregation was to call Tim to be their pastor. The congregational vote was also unanimously in support of the board's recommendation. He was officially inviting Tim to come back to Broad Street Church.

It would be very difficult to describe the mixed feelings that Tim and Laura experienced. At the very least, just knowing they'd been invited back to pastor the Broad Street Church eased the feelings of failure and rejection they'd been dealing with for years. At the same time, the idea of making themselves vulnerable again was very frightening. Should they really sell their nice home and move back to the parsonage?

Laura looked at Tim, shook her head, and said, "I can't believe we're going to do this."

"No one has said we are yet," Tim responded. "Rev. Jackson, we need some time to pray and talk about this. I'm sure you understand."

"Of course," Rev. Jackson responded. He prayed with them and left with a promise to call them in a week or so.

Tim and Laura did a lot of talking and praying that next week. One of their children was in college now, and the other, Kim, was a junior in high school. They had no idea what Kim would think about going back to Broad Street Church and moving back to the parsonage. They were somewhat surprised when she indicated she wouldn't mind. She'd kept in touch with some of her friends there, so it wouldn't be like moving to a totally new neighborhood. After about three days they knew without a doubt that the Lord was calling them back to Broad Street Church.

Tim called Rev. Jackson and told him they accepted the call. He submitted his resignation at the auto parts store, and they put their house on the market.

Tim and Laura went to meet with the church board at Broad Street. Some of the board members from eight years ago were still there. The board planned a homecoming service for Tim and Laura for their first Sunday. The service was followed with a delicious meal and many hugs. Tim and Laura felt they had come home.

Tim and Laura both felt, though, that there was unfinished business. About six months after their return to Broad Street, Tim called the pastor of the church that was started by those who left Broad Street years earlier.

"Pastor, you probably don't know me, but my name is Tim

Johnson," Tim started the conversation.

"Oh, yes, I know you, Pastor," Pastor Mark Miller responded. "You've just returned as pastor of Broad Street Church, right?"

"I guess word gets around, doesn't it?"

"That's for sure. What can I do for you?"

It would be interesting to know what went through the minds of those who left Broad Street Church eight years earlier when they heard Pastor Johnson was coming to speak to them.

"Well, Mark, I'd like to address your congregation. You know there was a split in our church a few years ago, and I believe the Lord is in the process of healing the wounds that occurred then. I don't feel like that process will be complete until I have a chance to address those who left our church eight years ago."

"I'm glad to hear that a healing process has started," Pastor Miller responded. "By all means you can address the congregation. When would you like to do that?"

They set a date for several weeks later.

Tim thought and prayed a great deal about what he would say. He called Rev. Jackson for his counsel and prayer support. He and Laura talked and prayed that he would have just the right words to say when the time came.

It would be interesting to know what went through the minds of those who left Broad Street Church eight years earlier when they heard Pastor Johnson was coming to speak to them. Some questioned the wisdom of Pastor Miller's decision to let him come. After all, there would be many people in the church who weren't around when the split occurred and would have no idea what he was talking about. Pastor Miller told them that he believed a healing process was underway by the Lord's guidance, and he was not about to stand in the way.

The agreed-upon day came. Tim was nervous about what he was going to say. At the same time, however, he was keenly aware that the Lord was with him as he rose to speak.

"I want to begin by thanking Pastor Miller for the opportunity to speak to you this morning. I believe that this morning is a significant step in a healing process the Lord has started in my life and the lives of our congregations.

"Most of you probably know that your church was started by a group of people who decided eight years ago that they wanted to start a new church. They were attending Broad Street Church at the time, and I was their pastor. I was totally unprepared for their announcement one Sunday morning that they were leaving our church. I had no idea then, and have none now, as to why they thought they had to do that.

"One of the reasons I'm here this morning is to ask your forgiveness for whatever I did that made you feel you had to leave our church. You're good people, and I'm sure you had good reasons for what you did.

"I also want to say to you, however, that the way you chose to do it caused me and my family great pain. Most of you know that I was so devastated by what happened that I left the pastorate for more than eight years. I wish you had come to talk with me about your frustrations; I believe we could have worked together to make things right.

"You probably know that the folks at Broad Street have now invited me back to be their pastor. Laura and I have accepted their gracious invitation. We feel like we've come home, and I thank the Lord for His healing in our lives.

"Before the healing can be complete, however, I think we need to take one more step. Our church would like to invite you to join us for an evening of thanksgiving and celebration. We want to thank the Lord together for His goodness to our churches and to celebrate our oneness in Christ. We'll all bring food and have a lot of good singing and good preaching. We trust you'll accept our invitation."

Pastor Miller rose and said, "Pastor Johnson, we'll happily accept your invitation and thank you for it with all our hearts."

And what a service they had!

BIBLIOGRAPHY

Augsburger, David W. 1992. *Conflict Mediation Across Cultures: Pathways and Patterns.* Louisville, Ky.: Westminster Press.

Brett, J. M., S. B. Goldberg, and W. W. Ury. 1990. "Designing Systems for Resolving Disputes in Organizations." *American Psychologist* 45: 162-70.

Bridges, William. 1997. *Building Bridges.* New York: Harper.

———. 1999. *Managing Transitions: Making the Most of Change.* New York: Random House.

Burns, James MacGregor. 1978. *Leadership.* New York: Harper.

Cedar, Paul. 1994. "The Cost of Conflict." *Moody* (April): 11-15.

Cosgrove, Charles H., and Dennis Hatfield. 1994. *Church Conflict: The Hidden Systems Behind the Fights.* Nashville: Abingdon Press.

Dane, Leila F. 1997. "Ethnic Identity and Conflict Transformation." *Peace Review* 9 (4) (December): 503-7.

Diamond, Louise. 1994. "Beyond Win/Win: The Heroic Journey of Conflict Transformation." Occasional paper No. 4. Washington, D.C.: Institute for Multi-Track Diplomacy (November)
< http://www.Colorado.edu/confict/transform/diamond.htm > .

French, Warren, and David Allbright. 1998. "Resolving a Moral Conflict Through Discourse." *Journal of Business Ethics* (January) [8 January 2001:
< http://proquest.umi.com/pqdlink >].

Friend, Howard. 1996. "Holding the Center." *The Other Side* (July-August): 17-19.

Graham, Pauline. 1998. "Saying 'No' to Compromise; 'Yes' to Integration." *Journal of Business Ethics* (July) [5 January 2001:
< http://proquest.umi.com/pqdlink >].

Gulbranson, Jeanne E. 1998. "The Ground Rules of Conflict Resolution." *Industrial Management* (May/June) [5 January 2001:
< http://proquest.umi.com/pqdlink >].

Halverstadt, Hugh F. 1991. *Managing Church Conflict.* Louisville, Ky.: Westminster Press.

Hauerwas, Stanley. 1981. *A Community of Character.* South Bend, Ind.: Notre Dame.

Hays, Richard B. 1996. *The Moral Vision of the New Testament.* San Francisco: Harper.

Jameson, Jessica Katz. 1999. "Toward a Comprehensive Model for the Assessment and Management of Intraorganizational Conflict." *International Journal of Conflict Management* (July) [4 January 2001:

< http://proquest.umi.com/pqdlink >].

Johnson, David W., and Frank P. Johnson. 1982. *Joining Together.* 2nd ed. Englewood Cliffs, N.J.: Prentice-Hall.

Kozan, M. Kamil. 1997. "Culture and Conflict Management: A Theoretical Framework." *International Journal of Conflict Management* (October) [8 January 2001: < http://proquest.umi.com/pqdlink >].

Kurzynski, M. J. 1998. "The Virtue of Forgiveness as a Human Resource Management Strategy." *Journal of Business Ethics* (January) [8 January 2001: < http://proquest.umi.com/pqdlink >].

Leas, Speed. 2001a. "The Basics of Conflict Management in Congregations." In *Conflict Management in Congregations.* Ed. David B. Lott. Bethesda, Md.: Alban Institute, 20-44.

———. 2001b. "Harvesting the Learning of Conflict Management." In *Conflict Management in Congregations.* Ed. David B. Lott. Bethesda, Md.: Alban Institute, 1-12.

———. 2001c. *Moving Your Church Through Conflict.* Bethesda, Md.: Alban Institute.

———. 2001d. "When Conflict Erupts in Your Church." In *Conflict Management in Congregations.* Ed. David B. Lott. Bethesda, Md.: Alban Institute, 15-19.

Lederbach, John Paul. 1989. "Director's Circle." *Conciliation Quarterly* 8 (3) (summer): 12-14 [22 May 2001: < http://www.colorado.edu/conflict/transform/lederbach.htm >].

Lott, David B., ed. 2001. *Conflict Management in Congregations.* Bethesda, Md.: Alban Institute.

Olson-Buchanan, Julie B., Fritz Drasgow, Philip J. Moberg, and Alan Mead. 1998. "Interactive Video Assessment of Conflict Resolution Skills." *Personnel Psychology* (spring), 1-24 [8 January 2001: < http://proquest.umi.com/pqdlink >].

Parsons, George D. 2001a. "Language of Caring Spoken Here." In *Conflict Management in Congregations.* Ed. David B. Lott. Bethesda, Md.: Alban Institute, 109-12.

———. 2001b. "Recovering from a Church Fight: Talking Across the Old Lines." In *Conflict Management in Congregations.* Ed. David B. Lott. Bethesda, Md.: Alban Institute, 106-8.

Parsons, George D., and Speed Leas. 2001. "Creative Tension in Congregational Life: Beyond Homeostasis." In *Conflict Management in Congregations.* Ed. David B. Lott. Bethesda, Md.: Alban Institute, 62-65.

Pneuman, Roy W. 2001. "Nine Common Sources of Conflict in Congregations." In *Conflict Management in Congregations.* Ed. David B. Lott. Bethesda, Md.: Alban Institute, 45-53.

Rendle, Gil. 2001. "The Illusion of Congregational 'Happiness.'" In *Conflict Management in Congregations.* Ed. David B. Lott. Bethesda, Md.: Alban Institute, 83-94.

"Should I Die on This Hill?" 1997. *Youthworker* (November/December), 30-37.

Stewart, David. 1998. "Power Play." *Group* (January/February), 26-28.

Tillich, Paul. 1954. *Love, Power, and Justice.* New York: Oxford University Press.

Ury, William. 1999. *Getting to Peace.* New York: Viking.

Westerhoff, Caroline A. 2001. "Conflict: The Birthing of the New." In *Conflict Management in Congregations.* Ed. David B. Lott. Bethesda, Md.: Alban Institute, 54-61.

"When Conflict Erupts in Your Church." 2001. In *Conflict Management in Congregations.* Ed. David B. Lott. Bethesda, Md.: Alban Institute, 15-19.

Whetten, David S., and Kim S. Cameron. 1998. *Developing Management Skills.* New York: Harper and Row.

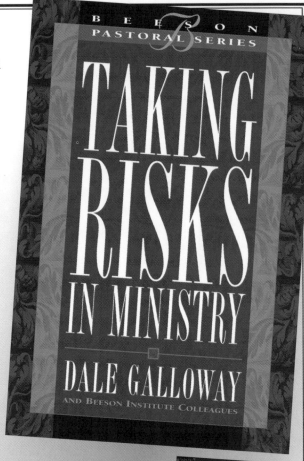
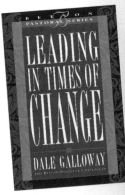

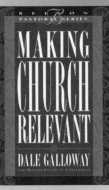